My Elders Taught Me

Aspects of Western Great Lakes American Indian Philosophy

John Boatman

American Indian Studies
University of Wisconsin–Milwaukee

UNIVERSITY
PRESS OF
AMERICA

D0963320

Lanham • New York • London

Copyright © 1992 by
University Press of America®, Inc.
4720 Boston Way
Lanham, Maryland 20706

3 Henrietta Street
London WC2E 8LU England

Library of Congress Cataloging-in-Publication Data

Boatman, John F., 1935–
My elders taught me : aspects of Western Great Lakes American
Indian philosophy / John Boatman.
p.   cm.
Includes bibliographical references.
1. Indians of North America—Great Lakes Region—Philosophy.
2. Indians of North America—Great Lakes Region—Religion and
mythology.   I. Title.
E78.G7B63   1992   191'.089'97—dc20   92–11965 CIP

ISBN 0–8191–8691–0 (cloth : alk. paper)
ISBN 0–8191–8692–9 (pbk. : alk. paper)

 The paper used in this publication meets the minimum requirements of
American National Standard for Information Sciences—Permanence
of Paper for Printed Library Materials, ANSI Z39.48–1984.

CONTENTS

□ □ □ □ □ □ □ □ □ □ □

PREFACE

In the nineteen years I have been teaching in the area of American Indian Studies at the university level, I have found that there are very few texts available which deal with the subject of Western Great Lakes American Indian philosophy from the perspective taught by American Indian Elders. Most of the available books are written by non-natives, who, never having experienced the living philosophy of tribal Elders, do not have a strong appreciation of or connection with the traditions they describe. In addition, many of these books, which contain a great deal of Eurocentric bias, are largely inaccurate from the perspective of the tribal peoples themselves.

I have written *My Elders Taught Me* from my perspective as an individual who was privileged to learn from several Western Great Lakes American Indian Traditional Elders.

Over a period of at least forty-five years, Beshagwawerie and Waubeeshans, Ojibway Elders from the islands between the Lower and Upper Peninsulas of Michigan, shared their memories with me. In the 1960's and 1970's my instructors included the Elders Pauees and Wallace Pyawasit of the Menominee American Indian Nation who officially recognized and accepted me in a traditional Naming Ceremony in 1976 at the Zoar village on the Menominee Indian Reservation in Wisconsin. The years of experiences with them and others taught me many things and motivated me to challenge some of the assertions of so-called scholars of the American Indian.

Pauees and Wallace Pyawasit died more than ten years ago. In this book I honor their spirits, and the spirits of the other Elders I have known, for accepting me as their student and sharing their knowledge.

In addition, I thank the herbalist, teacher, and medicine woman, Keewaydinoquay, an Elder of Chippewa and Odawa ancestry, for sharing important information with me over the years.

To all of these Elders, I am indebted and gratefully acknowledge their patient guidance.

I wish to thank Nancy O. Lurie, the present Curator of Anthropology at the Milwaukee Public Museum. From the time that she was one of my professors at the University of Wisconsin-Milwaukee, and throughout the nineteen years that I have taught here, she has continued to be both friend and advisor. Also, I am grateful to UWM Associate Dean G. Richard Meadows, who encouraged me and allowed me the time to write this book. Lastly I wish to acknowledge my dedicated editor, Carla Dorgay, for her diligence in working with me on the final draft of this book. Her writing skills and patience are most appreciated.

I dedicate this book to my children Colleen, Carolyn, and Michael, to my grandson John Michael Katchenago, to Craig and Karine, and to my wife Patricia without whose prodding, support, and understanding I would not have sat down to write.

INTRODUCTION

In this book I will examine various aspects of a selection of Western Great Lakes American Indian philosophical traditions and beliefs.

Philosophy includes several subdisciplines. The subdiscipline of metaphysics is concerned with questions about the fundamental nature of reality and 'being'. Metaphysics includes both cosmology and ontology. Cosmology considers how peoples perceive the nature and order (or disorder) of the universe while ontology considers questions relating to the types, natures, and relationships of beings in the universe.

The term "religion" encompasses the more or less institutionalized practices which relate to philosophic beliefs, particularly those involving service to and worship of a supernatural being or beings.

As I indicated in my preface, a number of scholars have written about the philosophical and religious beliefs and practices of Western Great Lakes American Indians. These include scholarly pioneers as well as more recent writers. Most of the writers were and are Europeans or United States Americans of European heritage. Many of them spent a relatively short amount of time, if any, doing fieldwork in American Indian communities. Their Eurocentric "world view"[1] of philosophical and religious matters influenced their interpretation of what they saw--or *thought* they saw. The result of this method of scholarship is similar to a translation in which the words may be correct but the meaning becomes altered by the perceptions of the translator. In the case of many published "studies" of American Indian philosophy, American Indian beliefs were translated through a Western European mind-set. The result is a work which reflects what the scholar and Cree Indian Emma LaRocque termed the "dichotomy of civilization versus savagery."[2]

A published work written within the context of this dichotomy is often perceived by the scholars who quote it to be a valuable source of information, although from the perspective of the American Indian peoples, it is an inaccurate source. Unfortunately, those authors who base their writings on these inaccurate works unknowingly incorporate a Eurocentric and often racist bias into the body of their own work. The problem is further complicated by authors who quote and cite scholars who have never spent any time doing fieldwork in the area that they write about. There are European scholars, based at European universities, whom scholars in the United States recognize as experts on American Indian philosophy and/or religions! The work of these European scholars, as well as that of their colleagues in the United States, is sometimes not only biased but grossly inaccurate.

The ethnocentric bias in most scholarly work about American Indian philosophy and/or religion is so pervasive and entrenched that many present-day scholars cannot perceive it and therefore deny that it exists. For this reason it is all the more important to focus upon works by American Indian writers such as Edward Benton-Banai and Basil Johnston whose understanding of American Indian philosophy and religion is based largely on first-hand experiences. These writers have an understanding that can only come from living within the philosophical framework of their ancestors. Their actual experiences give their works an authenticity not present in works by non-native writers who are unable to release themselves from the restrictions of their own sociocultural beliefs.

Any attempt to describe the philosophic and religious beliefs and practices of any group depends largely upon the world view of the individual who does the describing. If one tries to study aspects of American Indian philosophy and related ceremonial practices utilizing the world view of the European-American dominant society, one will only see what one *believes* is already there. Conversely, *one will not see that which one believes cannot be there.*

As Barre Toelken points out, "Before we can *see* we must *learn how to look.*"[3]

I question the validity of what many have used as primary sources because the European-American, Judeo-Christian ethnocentric bias may have significantly distorted the observations of the authors. For example, early European accounts of American Indian religious practitioners spread the belief that the native American people were the followers of "Satan" who directed and were in contact with powers emanating from hell. European observers came to this conclusion because the things they saw were so different from their own religious practices that they assumed such practices must be outside of the realm of the "true God."[4] I cite this example to stress the point that the authoritativeness of many works on American Indian philosophy is dependent upon what the observer perceives as real and not upon what the participant actually perceives and experiences.

Illuminating the discrepancy between these two realities is a primary purpose for writing this book.

In this text I rely upon my own experiences of Western Great Lakes American Indian philosophic beliefs and related religious practices obtained under the guidance of American Indian Elders over the past forty-five years. I intend, in the light of what those tribal Elders taught me, to examine, analyze, challenge, and correct many of the misconceptions and errors which are so pervasive in the available scholarship on this subject.

My intention in this book is to *see* with the native eye--in so far as that is possible. I will demonstrate how the European-American ethnocentric world view distorted and still distorts the ability to understand the actual beliefs and practices of specific American Indian groups.

Even accounts by "traditional" contemporary American Indians, such as those of my now-deceased Elders, may be vulnerable to suggestions of relative inauthenticity. This is because for several generations the cultures preserved in the living memory of various Elders have been so denigrated and oppressed by members of the dominant society that unwanted and perhaps even unnoticed changes occurred in both beliefs and practices. American Indian tribal peoples, and especially those in the Great Lakes region, generally developed adaptive strategies when confronted with the significant and rapid changes following European intrusion in the Americas. In the process, change occurred in both beliefs and practices. In societies based upon an oral tradition, one is not able to "stop-motion" and "fix" upon a particular belief or practice stating that it is (or is not) "the traditional way."

My focus in this text, whenever possible, is on that segment in time which my principal teachers, the Elders, recalled either personally or through legend.

To most individuals in our society, such things as talking to plants or being spiritually influenced by the forces of the winds and the night are perceived as being outside of normalcy, as absurd, as having no rationale or logic, and as being outside of the logical, intellectual framework of what is 'true'.

We find that the European-American world view stresses the domination of *man* over nature and the subjugation of the Earth Mother to such an extent that destruction of the planet's ability to sustain life as we know it appears imminent.

Some may find that the information in this book, including the various legends, stories, and other teachings of the Elders, is similar to information found in the all too few books by other American Indians on this subject. This is because various tribal Elders often told similar stories and legends, teaching much the same ontology and cosmology no matter from which tribe or geographical region of the country they happened to be. There is no conscious intent on my part to violate any other writer's copyright.

Some American Indian readers may find that the information presented in this book is somewhat different, perhaps vastly different, from what they learned in their own family or tribe. Some may even take the position that what I have written is wrong. I ask these individuals to bear in mind that this book contains only that which my significant Elders taught me. It may be prudent to leave the decision regarding what is right and what is wrong to those in the Spirit-World.

In this book I will bring the teachings of my Elders into focus and invite scholars and students to experience an alternative philosophy that opens "doors" onto a panoramic world view. This is an introduction to a living philosophy which, I believe, may be essential to a generation dependent upon the balance of both Nature and the Earth for its very survival.

NOTES

1. "A comprehensive conception of the world from a specific standpoint." *Webster's Ninth New Collegiate Dictionary*, 1987 ed.

2. Jennifer S. H. Brown and Robert Brightman, *"The Orders of the Dreamed": George Nelson on Cree and Northern Ojibwa Religion and Myth, 1823*, (St. Paul: Minnesota Historical Society Press, 1988), 199.

3. Barre Toelken, "Seeing With a Native Eye: How Many Sheep Will It Hold?" in *Seeing With a Native Eye: Essays on Native American Religion*, ed. W. H. Capps, (New York: Harper and Row, 1976), 24. My emphasis.

4. Although the native peoples believed in neither "Satan" nor "hell."

CHAPTER ONE
SETTING THE STAGE: FROM ANOTHER PERSPECTIVE

For some readers the concepts contained within this book may be somewhat familiar--if only perhaps on an intuitive level. For many others this book will provide a conceptual orientation that seems quite alien from the perspective of their own cultural background.

The reader is asked to bear in mind that education is the process of apprehending and examining new ideas, of sifting through and winnowing them, and finally incorporating those that may be useful into one's own storehouse of knowledge.

One of my friends likes to tell a story about a man who dreamt he was a butterfly. In the dream the man fluttered here and there and was quite content. Suddenly, he woke up. Remembering the dream, he wondered, "Who am I *really*? Am I a human who dreamt I was a butterfly? Or, am I a butterfly still dreaming that I am human?"

When asked what that story had to do with the teachings of our Elders, my friend responded, "A rock is a rock, and a tree is a tree, and do not ask why. Think!" We often expect to be given answers to questions without taking the time to see whether we already have the answers within ourselves. Often the task of the Elders is to help us remember things we may already know, but have somehow forgotten.

The Elders stressed that the answers to sometimes difficult but meaningful questions must come from within. Even more importantly, they said that one will never arrive at different answers unless one is able to ask different questions.

This book provides the reader with material which may provoke different questions. As Clyde Kluckhohn and Dorothea Leighton point out so well in their book, *The Navajo*, "the pie of experience can be sliced in all sorts of ways."[1] Thomas W. Overholt and J. Baird Callicott added that the commonly accepted, essentially Western European and European-American "way" of slicing the pie is not the only "true" and correct "way."[2]

In this book we will slice the pie differently so that readers may discover new ways of asking questions waiting to be answered.

Webster's Ninth New Collegiate Dictionary defines "truth" in part as, "the property of being in accord with fact or reality." One might ask, which facts and whose reality? Is there only one "truth?"

Perhaps in the attempt to discover the nature of "truth" and its relationship to "reality," one should take a look through "doors" previously unknown or believed to be locked or closed. In the quest for knowledge, one should decide for one's self what is "true" and what is "real."

At the beginning of such a quest, when trying both to decide which road to take and to discover the appropriate "door" which will open onto that road, remember that there may be unknown "doors" within ourselves. We must learn to look inside as well as outside; that is, spend time in reflection as well as in observation. By doing so we are then prepared to continue to the place where the four roads run side by side. Here, we must choose the middle road and walk along it while seeing with the physical eyes closed.[3] It is when we are on the middle road, walking with eyes closed, that the truth will reveal itself.

Western Science, which to a great extent provides our cultural orientation in the twentieth century, has its initial beginnings in the metaphysics of the early Greeks, who in turn adopted many concepts from the ancient Egyptians. Interestingly, some Egyptian and Greek philosophers believed, as did many of the ancient American Indians, that all matter is (or was) "alive." They usually made no distinction between the notions of animate and inanimate objects, nor between the notions of spirit and matter. They saw all forms of existence as being endowed with life and spirit within a universe that was a kind of colossal organism created and supported by a cosmic "force" in the state of eternal "becoming." This state of eternal "becoming" is the expression of the dynamic and cyclic interplay of positive and negative forces contained within and manifested throughout a cosmic unity: a unity in which the sum of opposing forces transcends each force in and of itself.

Later philosophical and intellectual development in Western Europe, influenced largely by the spread of Christianity, led many scholars to make a clear distinction between the concepts of spirit and matter. Matter was then viewed as being made up of normally passive "dead parts" comprising a "material world" which would soon become the sole domain of Western Science. Questions relating to the spirit and the Spirit-World were relegated to a separate discipline: philosophy. Over time, anything relating to the Spirit-World became, in the view of many scientists, a figment of the inadequately informed (or completely uninformed) imagination.

More and more the universe was thought of as a huge machine-like entity. The earlier view of a dynamic and organic universe driven by constant interrelations between spirit and matter survived by and large only in the religions of the aboriginal peoples of the earth who were, in comparison to Western ideals, thought of as unsophisticated, uncivilized, and perhaps even savage.

Meanwhile, the Western European "sophisticates," with their mechanistic world view, perceived of the notion of "space" as an unchangeable absolute. They believed that any observable changes in the physical world could be defined in terms of a separate dimension which they called "time." Time was considered to be like a flowing river, moving from the past, through the present, into the future.

In the early twentieth century, however, two separate developments, relativity theory and quantum physics, shattered confidence in scientific certainty and radically changed the Western perception of the universe. Ironically, it seems that Western beliefs are now coming full circle.

In light of these current theories, many scholars believe that we may have much to learn by reexamining the ideas of the ancient thinkers.

Relativity theory includes the hypothesis that space is not simply a three-dimensional construct and that time is not a separate dimensional entity. Instead, space and time are viewed as intimately interconnected, forming the four-dimensional continuum of space-time. This is precisely the same view held by the ancient philosophers discussed earlier, including the American Indians.

Quantum physics posits that there is a basic 'oneness' inherent to the universe that is intimately involved with the space-time continuum and is both governed by and dependent upon an over-riding and under-lying force of pure energy.

The Elders, who viewed the universe in the same manner, said that this 'oneness' of the universe is expressed by a plus-symbol (+) which they called the "Four Winds Cross." It is a symbol of universal balance. The vertical bar represents the transcendence and the 'oneness' which is inherent between the readily observable physical world and its transcendent source in the Spirit-World. The horizontal bar represents "the One," permeating and inter-linking "the many," which thereby interconnects all observable and non-observable phenomena in the universe. The ancient Western Great Lakes American Indian philosophers called this transcendent and unifying force "Gitchi Manitou" or "Great Spirit," who is the source of the eternal cosmic heartbeat.

The proponents of relativity theory and quantum physics hypothesize that events which we perceive to take place in the past, present, and future are actually separated into these categories by our finite and three-dimensionally perceiving minds. As a result, time appears to flow like a river: always traveling in the same direction. From the perspective of the space-time continuum, however, these time divisions are artificial and do not exist as separate entities; the past is the present is the future in an eternally manifesting "now." Time continually returns upon itself in an interconnecting spiral. *Time is cyclic.* By looking into space we even may be able to look backward in time.

Reality is continually and simultaneously "unfolded," so to speak, through the manifestation of a transcendent "force"; however, this "unfolding" is perceived by our finite minds as happening sequentially. Our brains appear to mathematically construct a functional reality by interpreting those energy frequencies within time and space which transcend our limited ability to apprehend them. These frequencies are transformed into a concrete and sequential language that allows us to "make sense" out of the dynamic and complex forces at work in the continuum of space and time. Consequently, we only get glimpses of the reality of the space-time continuum. In some experiential situations defined as "paranormal," the glimpse is blurred, as it were, and we are able to momentarily perceive the synchronicity of events taking place in our universe. Taken in this context, it is possible that some of the so-called mystic experiences which people have reported since ancient times do make some kind of scientific "sense."

What are called *paranormal* or *psychic (PSI) phenomena* may take place when the human brain somehow gains access to information stored in a dimension existing beyond our limited perception of the space-time continuum.

Physics has opened "doors" onto many areas of reality which are often imperceptible to the ordinary human senses. Some examples of these imperceptible forces which nonetheless have a profound influence upon our lives include electricity, radio and television signals, inertia, momentum, and gravity. We can perceive the results of these invisible forces but we cannot normally "see" them. In much the same manner, PSI phenomena may be thought of as the result of experiencing manifestations from an unseen "energy force."

Some physicists have begun to investigate PSI phenomena seriously. It has already been over eleven years since Brian Josephson, a Nobel Laureate in Physics from Cambridge University in England, stated that he was ninety-nine percent convinced of the reality of PSI events.[4]

PSI phenomena, and experiences relating to the action of PSI phenomena, have been reported by American Indians since ancient times. As the reader will soon find, the Elders did not use the contemporary terms to describe these phenomena; nevertheless, almost all were known to the Elders by different names. For the sake of clarity, the explanations on the following pages will refer to these phenomena in contemporary terminology rather than by their various American Indian names.[5]

Two major forms of PSI phenomena are *extrasensory perception (ESP)*, which is a receptive, informational phenomenon, and *psychokinesis (PK)*, which is an expressive phenomenon.

ESP includes *telepathy*: an apparent awareness of information and/or emotions existing within, and possibly emanating from, another individual. Telepathy is often thought of as mind-to-mind communication. It occurs spontaneously and quite often when one least expects it. Another type of *ESP* is *clairvoyance*: the ability to "know" things about particular persons by focusing on an object or location associated with them. It usually manifests as visions, sounds, or smells obtained without actually using the eyes, ears, or nose. Clairvoyance is accompanied by the feeling of being outside of the physical body.

Sometimes information obtained through various forms of ESP may be about events which have not yet taken place in a linear segment of "normal" time. In those cases the perceptive ability is called *precognition*. At other times information may be obtained about events which took place in the past. In those cases the ability is called *retrocognition*.

Researchers hypothesize that most, perhaps all, material objects are somehow able to "record" information in the electromagnetic field that surrounds all matter. It appears that some individuals have the ability to "decode" this "recorded" information from the energy field.

The second major type of PSI phenomena, *psychokinesis* (*PK*), is often described as effecting the process of "mind over matter" in which the mind influences the energy field of material objects or physical processes without the use of any apparent physical force. Psychokinesis includes the ability to move objects from a distance (*telekinesis*), and the ability to move objects from one location to another without the objects having been observed actually traveling the physical distance (*teleportation*). The ability to put impressions on film, video, or sound tapes without touching them, as well as the process of healing without administering any substances and without apparently physically altering the patient, are also forms of psychokinesis.

A *poltergeist* is recurrent spontaneous psychokinesis. This phenomenon includes unusual movements or sounds which appear to be brought about by the mind of a particular human being who lives in the location where the poltergeist activity is taking place. This phenomenon typically lasts a limited amount of time--a few weeks to a year or so at the most. A poltergeist is believed to be created by the subconscious thought and energy projections of a human being who is in an extremely stressful, tense, and frustrating situation or relationship. In such cases, these individuals react subconsciously rather than consciously, and the result is a psychokinetic outburst--a PK temper-tantrum.

Hauntings are still another type of PSI phenomenon. As stated previously, it appears that all material objects somehow "record" information in the electromagnetic energy field that surrounds all matter. Hauntings occur when individuals who are able to decode the recorded information (often without intending to do so or being conscious of the fact that they are doing so) pick up the information recorded at any given location. This may involve the perception of electromagnetic traces of humans who previously lived in the location. Researchers have noted that variables such as certain times of the day, moon phases, etc., affect the "play-back" ability of the "recording," and can either inhibit or exacerbate it. Hauntings are not, as is commonly believed, the same thing as apparitions.

Apparitions are manifestations caused by the continued presence on earth of the ghost-portion of an individual's Spirit after the death of the physical body. Researchers have found little evidence of any harm associated with these phenomena, except in some cases where a poltergeist manifestation is also taking place. In cases where harm is caused, it is caused by *Discarnate Entities*, who never take on a physical form, rather than by "ghosts."

The reader is reminded that even though these ideas may appear to be rather strange, or perhaps even unbelievable, it is important to bear in mind that the Western Great Lakes American Indian peoples did believe that these phenomena, called by other names, were real. As their philosophy developed, awareness of these phenomena provided a means of answering questions which helped define their notions of "reality" and "truth" within the context of a dynamic and ever-changing universe.

NOTES

1. Clyde Kluckhohn and Dorothea Leighton, *The Navajo*, (Garden City: Doubleday and Co., 1962), 254.

2. Thomas W. Overholt and J. Baird Callicott, *Clothed-In-Fur And Other Tales: An Introduction To An Ojibwa World View*, (Washington, D.C.: University Press of America, 1982), 13.

3. Dennis Tedlock and Barbara Tedlock, *Teachings From The American Earth: Indian Religion and Philosophy*, (New York: Liveright, 1975), xxiii., 116.

4. *Science Digest*, September-October 1980, pp. 84-87, 116.

5. For a much more detailed explanation and treatment of the phenomenon, the reader may wish to consult Lloyd Auerbach's *ESP, Hauntings, and Poltergeists*, (New York: Warner, 1986). At the time he wrote the book, Auerbach was on the faculty at Kennedy University in Orinda, California.

CHAPTER TWO
THE ATISOKANAK WORLD

This chapter explains ancient beliefs and concepts which relate to twentieth century scientific explanations about energy and life in the universe. These concepts may also offer new insights into assertions made by scholars about the philosophical beliefs and related practices of Western Great Lakes American Indians.

The concept of what I have chosen to call the *Atisokanak World* requires particular attention by the reader because it encompasses many ideas which may seem alien in the late twentieth century when much of our ability to perceive the omnipresent cycles of the natural world is blinded by the sociocultural milieu in which we live.

THE TERM ATISOKANAK WORLD

Throughout this book I have chosen to use the term Atisokanak World to describe a multi-dimensional energy "world" which is the originating point of all "power," and which includes special types of beings whom I call *Atisokanak Persons*. From the perspective of this metaphysics, these entities actually exist; they are not mythological beings despite the fact that some scholars are inclined to characterize them as such.[1] The Atisokanak World is the place where the Atisokanak Persons abide. Basil Johnston, the Ojibway scholar, referred to this place by the name "Cheebi-akeeng," or "land of the soul-spirits."[2]

SUPREME BEING

In the introduction to this text I highlighted the problems with the European/ American way of *seeing* Western Great Lakes American Indian philosophical beliefs and related practices. Based upon inaccurate observations, writers often assumed that American Indians in this area believed in and worshipped many deities--that they were polytheistic. These writers are very wrong. As a consequence of this misconception, it is not uncommon to find sources which reduce the complex American Indian belief system to a simplistic mythology by misrepresenting various Atisokanak Persons as the different "gods" of some nonexisting American Indian pantheon.

The Western Great Lakes American Indian peoples are *monotheistic*. They have always believed in one Supreme Being called "Gitchi Manitou" or "Great Spirit," who is the primary source of existence. "In the beginning," the Elders said, "only Great Spirit existed." The Elders taught that Gitchi Manitou is both the Creator and Prime Sustainer whose cosmic identity is *both female and male*. Great Spirit is the source of continually manifesting positive and negative energies that must be maintained in a balanced state. As the source of these energies, Great Spirit embodies the absolute potentiality for *all* that manifests into 'being'. According to the Elders, all that Gitchi Manitou *dreamed* came into 'being'.

Louis Hennepin, a seventeenth century missionary priest, understood the American Indian concept of the Great Spirit when he wrote in 1683: "the Indians had an idea of a 'Master of Life.' "[3]

Others who recorded in writing the belief in the One Supreme Being include Andrew J. Blackbird, an Ottawa Leader from Michigan, and John C. Wright, also of Ottawa ancestry. Blackbird, who received a European-style education and later worked as a U. S. Government interpreter, wrote in a book published in 1887, "Ottawa and Chippewa Indians...believed that there is a Supreme Ruler of the Universe, the Creator of all things, the Great Spirit, to whom [they] offer worship and sacrifices."[4] Thirty years later Wright also emphasized the important role of the Great Spirit as Creator and Supreme Ruler, "...first man [was] created by the Gitchi Manitou [who was] the Ruler of Creation."[5]

Further evidence that American Indians were monotheistic comes from John M. Cooper, who wrote the following in 1934: "That there was but one Supreme Being is reasonably clear from the evidence....The Supreme Being was consistently conceived of as being somewhere above [the Earth plane]...."[6] Cooper concluded, "*All informants* agreed that the Supreme Being was really the master or 'boss' of things in general, including mankind."[7]

Part of the reason that many scholars insist upon claiming that American Indians were polytheistic is because they can support their claims with the works of early writers who observed the "worship of spirits" and then incorrectly concluded that instead of worshipping a single supreme deity, American Indians called upon many smaller deities for assistance in the daily tasks essential for sustenance. These scholars cite the French Catholic missionary Claude Allouez, who worked among tribal people in the Oconto and Green Bay areas of Wisconsin during the last decades of the seventeenth century. Allouez stated, "Whatever seems to them either helpful or hurtful they call a Manitou (spirit), and pay it the worship and veneration which we render only to the true God."[8] This is an illustration of the failure of the non-native observer to understand that American Indians venerated beings other than the Supreme Being in much the same manner that some Christians venerate angels and saints. These beings (manitos) were often considered guardian spirits. The Elders who were my teachers would agree with John Cooper's observation that, "The Supreme

Being was conceived of quite clearly as distinct from the...guardian spirits...."[9]

Unfortunately, many of the contemporary scholars who write about American Indian philosophy and related practices dismiss the statements of contemporary American Indian Elders, choosing instead to believe Europeans and European-Americans whose early journals provide "evidence" which fits their hypotheses.

Because of the nature of oral traditions, and also as a result of the influence of missionaries, traders, and other Europeans who came into the Western Great Lakes American Indian territories, my Elders acknowledged that there has been influence "from the outside" upon their tradition. In spite of those influences, however, their basic philosophy concerning the Supreme Being remains unchanged.

I find it very important to stress the existence of the One Great Spirit because this is one of the principal truths of traditional Western Great Lakes American Indian metaphysics. The Great Spirit who manifests into 'being' both the Spirit-World and the many Now-Worlds is the source of *everything*, known and unknown, in the universe.

It appears that those scholars who do not accept the teachings of the tribal Elders regarding a pre-European belief in a Supreme Being cannot (or will not) accept these teachings because they have been taught to *see* only that which they expect to find. As a result, they did not *see* what was actually there!

POWER

"Power" is an *amoral, amorphous, both positive and negative energy force* which pervades the universe. It is innate to and emanates only from the Atisokanak World. "Power" may manifest into a Now-World only as a result of Atisokanak-initiated action. It may manifest in two ways: directly into the Now-World, or through Now-World beings serving as conduits. These conduits may be human.

No human (or any other Now-World being for that matter) has any inherent power. When we "have power" we are actually only conduits for an energy force over which the Great Spirit has ultimate control.

All Now-World females are designated by Great Spirit as potential *automatic* conduits. They must, however, first learn how to become proper and effective conduits so that they will use their ability appropriately and in a balanced manner.

Males may be chosen by Great Spirit to be conduits, but this is considered to be quite rare. In order for most males even to become potential conduits, they must seek the development of a meaningful relationship with the Atisokanak World and the Atisokanak Persons. Ordinarily this relationship is initiated at the time of the puberty Vision Quest. These "special" males must also learn to use their ability properly. If either a female or a male uses the gift of being a conduit improperly, it could (and according to the Elders often did) backfire to the detriment of the individual who misused the power and possibly imperil others close to the individual.

ATISOKANAK PERSONS

Three main types of beings inhabit the Atisokanak World: Discarnate Entities, Souls Previously Incarnate in a Now-World, and Life-Form Masters. These spirit-manifestations carry out the will of the all-powerful Great Spirit.

DISCARNATE ENTITIES

Discarnate Entities are spirit/energy-beings. These beings have never entered a Now-World in physical body form. There are two principal subtypes of Discarnate Entities.

The first subtype includes energy beings which will never take on any substantive material form. These entities may be either benevolent or malevolent in nature. The Elders cautioned that great care must be taken in dealing with any phenomenon which may be a manifestation of a discarnate entity because one may not know whether the entity is a manifestation of positive or of negative energy. The Elders considered the European concept of the incubus and succubus to be examples of this first subtype.

Souls which have not yet incarnated into a Now-World body comprise the second subtype of Discarnate Entities. All of the life-sustaining Souls that animate bodies in a Now-World originally come from this subtype. The Elders taught that for many life-forms, as is the case with humans, the Soul enters and animates the non-living matter at the instant of conception.

SOULS WHICH HAVE BEEN PREVIOUSLY INCARNATE

The Soul which has been incarnate at least once in a Now-World body is the second type of Atisokanak Person. Physicist and astronomer Gustaf Stromberg described ''Soul'' in a manner which is strikingly similar to the teachings of the tribal Elders.[10] Stromberg believed that there is no doubt about the existence of the human Soul, if we define it properly. He thought of it as a perceiving, feeling, willing, thinking, and remembering entity possessing a particular group of memories, most of which never rise to the level of consciousness. He explained that the memories are indelibly engraved in the electrical field of the brain. At the death of the physical brain, the brain-field, and the group of memories associated with it, contract in unchanged form and go back to the world from which they originally came; that is, the non-physical world of the abiding energy-field. According to Stromberg, the Soul is indestructible and immortal and carries with it an indelible record of all its memories and activities. Stromberg further points out that the lack of opportunities for adequate development during an incarnation within a physical body on Earth logically leads to the possibility of later incarnations either on Earth or other planets.

In a later work, Stromberg hypothesized that our real selves are our Souls, which belong before our birth and after our death to the non-physical energy world. He also believed that memories engraved in the Soul may produce a strong urge to make a new immersion into a physical world in an attempt to improve the record. This again introduces the possibility of reincarnation.[11]

The Elders taught that the Soul is the life-sustaining aspect of the Spirit. Each Now-World body has a Spirit within it while the body is alive. The Spirit consists of two aspects: the *Soul*, and the *Ghost*. If the body is to have life, the Soul aspect of the Spirit must remain within the body. At the instant the Soul aspect of the Spirit leaves the body, the body dies. It is, in fact, the departing of the Soul from the body which causes the body to die. The Soul, after leaving the body, travels for four days to reach the Atisokanak World. It may stay in the Atisokanak World or it may return to a Now-World.

Whether the Soul returns or not to a Now-World may depend upon the choice of the Soul or the judgement of the Atisokanak Life-Form Masters. Life-Form Masters may direct the Soul to return to a Now-World in the same type of form inhabited previously, or in a different form, in order to continue the realignment of positive and negative forces left unbalanced during other incarnations.

While the body is alive, the second aspect of the Spirit, the Ghost, is free to travel in and between the many Now-Worlds and into the Atisokanak World. This is called the *out-of-body-experience*. At the time of death, the Ghost aspect may or may not accompany the Soul to the Atisokanak World. The Ghost usually leaves within four days of the departure of the Soul, but sometimes it leaves much later. If the Ghost part of the Spirit remains in the Now-World after the Soul has left, phenomena referred to as *hauntings* or *apparitions* may occur.

The Ghost aspect travels outside of the body while the body is sleeping or in a trance state. The purpose of these travels is usually so that the ''dreamer'' may learn things deemed necessary to learn. The out-of-body-experience may have results which are either positive or negative in the spectrum of balance. Consequently, one was cautioned to be careful lest the pursuit of negative energies ''backfire'' on the pursuer. During the out-of-body-experience the Ghost may be anywhere in space and time and is able to change forms. This involves the concept of *metamorphosis*, which refers to the ability of both Atisokanak and Now-World Persons, including humans, to partially or completely alter their outward appearance for varying lengths of time. The change is never permanent. Now-World Persons require the assistance of an Atisokanak Person to accomplish this. An Atisokanak Person has the inherent ability to accomplish metamorphosis. Sometimes, depending upon circumstances, the change in a Now-World Person is neither consciously sought nor wanted.

The tribal Elders cautioned that one should always be cognizant of possible encounters with metamorphosed Atisokanak Persons. This possibility had to be taken into consideration in both waking and sleeping situations, including Dreams and Visions. If one simply accepts what appears to be obvious, either a great opportunity may be missed or the consequences could be more serious and result in some type of misfortune. The Elders cautioned, ''What you *see* might not be what is really there!''

There is an old and widespread belief that some individuals, with Atisokanak permission and assistance, assume different forms to pursue various activities. "Fireballs" and "bears" are forms commonly associated with the accomplishment of negative-serving tasks. When someone takes the form of a bear, it is sometimes referred to as Bear-Walking. Humans were cautioned from an early age to be very careful about accepting the outward appearance of things because, as I have already stated, what one thinks one "sees" with the physical eyes may in truth be something entirely different.

Before leaving the discussion about the concept of Soul, I feel it is imperative to take issue with the scholars who assert that American Indians, including those of the Western Great Lakes area, believed in a concept termed *soul dualism*. The concept implies that an individual has two Souls. This is not accurate! As I have explained, there are two aspects to the Spirit; however, this is not the same as having two separate Souls. There is no evidence which supports the theory of soul dualism as being applicable to the Western Great Lakes American Indians. It is in fact a misconception borne out of faulty translation. Some English speakers use the words "ghost," "soul," and "spirit" almost interchangeably; however, in most of the Western Great Lakes American Indian languages, these words have separate and distinct meanings. I first turn to the renowned pioneering linguistic work of R. R. Baraga, who compiled a dictionary of the Ojibway language in the mid-1800's. He included two separate words for the two aspects of the Spirit: "otchitchagoma," meaning "Soul," and "tchibai" (pronounced jii-bay), meaning "Ghost."[12] These words correspond to the concepts of Soul and Ghost as discussed on the previous pages of this book. To end, I hope, further conjecture about the verity and applicability of the concept of soul dualism, I cite the contemporary Ojibway scholar Basil Johnston, who explained the concept of the Spirit in terms of two functions: "One function was to sustain life and existence; the other to fulfill other purposes. In sleep that [first] *aspect* of the soul-spirit that was to sustain and maintain life remained conjoined to the body. The other [aspect] was free either to remain or leave."[13]

LIFE-FORM MASTERS

A third type of Atisokanak Person is the *Life-Form Master*, a Spirit archetype serving as the nurturing caretaker and overseer of all life-forms in the Now-Worlds. Each species in each Now-World has a separate and distinct Atisokanak World Life-Form Master. An individual member of a particular species contains essential elements of that Life-Form Master. Now-World Spirits contain some of the essence of their Atisokanak prototype.

The Elders taught that one should not alienate the Life-Form Masters of any species, and in particular any species normally sought for food, for fear that the Life-Form Master of that species would make hunting and fishing difficult or impossible in times of need. For this reason, one must respectfully ask the permission of the Life-

Form Master *before the hunt*, and particularly *before any kill*. One was cautioned to resort to killing *only when there was a bonafide need*. To deliberately alienate another life-form is to be out of balance with Great Spirit's intention and obliges the individual to do all that is necessary to attain balance once again.

While some Life-Form Masters have more "power" potential than others, according to their place in the inherent Atisokanak hierarchy, the Elders stressed that it is ultimately the Great Spirit who allows or does not allow events to occur.

RELATIONSHIP OF TRIBAL LEGENDS TO THE ATISOKANAK

The Elders taught that many of the tribal legends and stories were about *real events* that occurred in the distant past, involving *real persons* who were no longer alive in a Now-World body at the time when the story was first told. Their Souls are very much alive, however, in the Atisokanak World, unless presently reincarnated in a Now-World.

The individuals involved in the stories, often referred to as "Grandmothers" and "Grandfathers," have a great amount of "power" potential. Because they can travel into a Now-World from the Atisokanak World, the telling and retelling of their stories is thought to be a potential invitation, or perhaps even an invocation, for these Souls to come into the Now-World where their story is being told.

Since the Elders knew that some of the ancient stories involved mischievous, or even malevolently inclined individuals, the Elders exercised great caution in telling these stories. Certain stories were reserved for the very coldest portions of winter when it was thought to be less likely that potentially mischievous or negatively inclined "persons" would choose to travel from the Atisokanak World to the Now-World of the story teller.

Some stories sound somewhat fanciful or even confusing. This is because so much time has passed since the event actually took place. The stories, being subject to the natural frailties of human memory, and often retold with a different instructional emphasis, change with each telling. Nevertheless, if we learn how to *see*, we can find the truth within the seemingly fantastic events of these stories.

ATISOKANAK HIERARCHY

The Great Spirit created the Atisokanak World and established a hierarchy within it. As a result, not all Atisokanak Persons are equal in rank, nor do they have equal "power" potential. Among those who possess the greatest "power" potential are the Atisokanak Persons called the *Thunderers*.

THE THUNDERERS

In many Western Great Lakes American Indian languages, the Thunderers are

called "Animikeeg." They sometimes manifest in the Now-Worlds as clouds, lightning, and various loud noises related to storm conditions. The Elders said the
Thunderers could also manifest in the form of eagles. Eagles are thought to be very
special Now-World birds who serve as messengers between other Now-World Persons and the Thunderers. These messages would then reach the Great Spirit through
the Animikeeg. *Thunderers are not the same thing as Thunderbirds.* More will be said
about Thunderbirds in the chapter about the Star People.

HIEROPHANIES

These are special Atisokanak "passageways" which connect the Atisokanak
World with Now-Worlds. The Great Spirit designed the hierophanies to be two-way
places of passage. They are sometimes called gateways, or doorways, or simply doors.

The *hierophanies* are located at rather special, often wondrous, natural places in
the Now-Worlds such as hilltops, forest areas, special trees, islands, caves, and
waterfalls.

Manifestations from the Atisokanak World are believed to be particularly strong at
hierophanies, and clear perception of these manifestations is likely at such locations.

Easier passage through the doorways is possible at specific times; for instance,
during moon phase maximums and at dawn and dusk. During the solstices, equinoxes,
and certain other times, the hierophanies are also more permeable than they are at
other times of the year.

A Now-World Person can only use the hierophanies with the permission of
Atisokanak Persons. The Ghost aspect of the person's Spirit does the traveling through
the passageway while the Now-World Person is alive in a Now-World body.

Passage from a Now-World, such as Earth, into the Atisokanak World is assisted
or prevented by special Atisokanak Guardians, called *doorkeepers* or *gatekeepers*,
many of whom are powerful female beings.

The Elders taught that one should reverently "put down" (give) offerings at these
special places to honor the gatekeepers.

ATISOKANAK GIFTS AND METAPHYSICAL RECIPROCITY

Atisokanak Persons may choose to bestow telekinetic, psychokinetic, clairvoyant,
curative, or other parapsychological abilities upon Now-World Persons. These abilities are considered gifts, and when one consciously accepts these gifts, a correspond-
ing responsibility ensues. The Atisokanak giver expects and sometimes demands
reciprocal behavior from the recipient/acceptor. The Atisokanak giver defines what is
and what is not acceptable reciprocal behavior.

Usually, the Now-World beneficiary of the gift is expected to perform special acts
that will ritually honor the Atisokanak giver. The beneficiary may reverently lay down

or burn *Kinnikinnick*, a tobacco-like offering whose name means "much mixed."

Elders would caution against accepting Atisokanak gifts too quickly with the reminder that these special gifts come with considerable reciprocal responsibilities. With this in mind, the Elders taught that it is permissible to respectfully *attempt* to decline the gift.

Now-World beings, including humans, are also cautioned that the use of parapsychological abilities, and the commitments to the Atisokanak World implicit in their use, are "mirrored" and bound in the Atisokanak World. Improper use of these abilities reverberates throughout the Atisokanak World and may upset the balance of positive and negative forces. *Caution*, therefore, is the guide word.

POSSESSION AND CONTROL

According to the Elders, an Atisokanak Person or Persons may "possess" and "control" an individual when contact between the Atisokanak World and Now-Worlds takes place. A Now-World Person must maintain vigilance in order to avoid being possessed and controlled by negatively inclined Atisokanak beings.

During a *possession*, one or more Atisokanak Persons use a Now-World Person's body for varying lengths of time in order to facilitate Atisokanak interaction with other human beings. Possession often initially occurs when a Now-World Person's body is quite young, ill, or experiencing trauma. Involuntary metamorphosis (a temporary partial or total change in outward appearance) may occur during possession.

When faced with the probability of possession by a malevolent Atisokanak Person, one must ask positive and benevolently inclined Atisokanak-Guardians to intervene in order to release the individual from the negative influence. If one does not do this, or if one does not seek an Elder to assist in doing this, or if one is too young or ill to do this, the possession may continue throughout much of the lifetime of the body.

A possession does *not* have to be an inherently negative experience. Some great healers allow themselves to be possessed in order to channel special powers from the Atisokanak World.

EMOTION IN ATISOKANAK/NOW-WORLD RELATIONSHIPS

Atisokanak Persons are affected quite easily by the emotions of Now-World Persons. The Elders taught that one should be aware of one's emotions lest they attract undesirable Atisokanak attention.

The Elders particularly stressed the need for understanding and dealing with the emotion of fear. They taught that fear feeds on the energy of the one who creates it. Fear must be faced, properly dealt with, and disposed of so that it will not incapacitate the individual by creating a situation in which the individual must constantly replenish the energy that fear consumes.

PSYCHIC EXTENSIONS

The Elders warned that one should be careful when disposing of one's hair, nails, blood, and spittle, lest harm should befall an individual as a result of someone else misusing and/or abusing these items.

TIME

Time from the perspective of Western Great Lakes American Indian metaphysics is *not* linear; it is cyclic, interwoven, and interconnecting in a spiraling and constantly manifesting space-time continuum with no distinct differences between past, present, and future. In cyclic time, a related concept called *Mawandji*, or "Remembering into the Future," is possible. This in turn is related to an understanding of karma and reincarnation.

KARMA AND REINCARNATION

Karma, although a non-American Indian term, is an apt term to describe the phenomenon which involves the springing-back into harmonious balance of the elastic-like universe whenever that balance is disturbed. It is a multidimensional and nonlinear phenomenon.

In order to maintain 'balance', old patterns recorded in the energy field are re-played so that positive corrective changes can be inserted in their place.

This is where *reincarnation* plays a crucial role. As I have stated previously, when an individual in a Now-World dies, it is possible for the Soul part of the Spirit to return to the Now-World and actively function in another Now-World body. This most often occurs when important tasks were left unfinished in other lifetimes or when grievous wrongs occur which tend toward the negative side of the spectrum of balance. Karma functions to bring into balance business left unfinished or not corrected. Since it works in cyclic time, *all* actions impact upon a single lifetime.

Quite often those with whom we have had close ties in the "past" will reappear in "present" situations. It is the functioning of karma which continually draws us into environments and relationships where old patterns are replayed until completed in a manner which enhances the balance of energies in the universe.

During a reincarnation, the Now-World body has more than one Soul functioning within it. It has a previously not-incarnated Soul and an Old-Soul (or possibly Souls if more than one Old-Soul is functioning within the same body). This may lead to behavioral symptoms which some mental health practitioners call Multiple-Personality Syndrome.

The Elder Keewaydinoquay said this about the previously incarnated Soul:

When a spirit enters the cycle of life on this earth, no one knows if it is [the Soul's] first cycle or [its] forty-second cycle, that is not of importance here. What is important? That [the individual's] feet be placed upon the Sun Trail...and that this trail [of life] be walked with Honor....[W]hen the Drum speaks, the pattern vibrates, singing out...the importance of the path of honor through this cycle.[14]

MANITOS: SPECIAL SPIRIT-BEINGS

Special Spirit-Beings are called manitos, or manidos. They are all created by the Great Spirit, Gitchi Manitou, who controls their actions.

A significant number of these Spirit-Beings are interactively involved with Now-World beings. Human beings often seek relationships with manitos such as the Guardian Spirit, who is sought and may appear during the puberty Vision Quest. There are other manitos who are regarded with dread and avoided if possible.

The Elders taught that humans should not expect too much from manitos nor should they take for granted or abuse a relationship with a manito, otherwise a manito might hurt the abusive human.

Some scholars contend that human existence depended upon one's ability to establish and maintain relationships with manitos. This is *not* correct. According to the Elders, the Western Great Lakes tribal peoples believed that _the ultimate source of existence was the one Great Spirit, Gitchi Manitou_. Some scholars have even gone so far as to write that it was the duty of the manitos to keep human beings alive and healthy. That is nonsense! Manitos can and do help keep humans alive and healthy by interceding on their behalf with Great Spirit, as well as by watching over, guiding, and protecting them and other Now-World beings. Nevertheless, it is not their duty! Manitos are powerful Atisokanak beings, and as such, they are much more powerful than humans and therefore not duty-bound to them. They do help humans, if re-quested--and if they are so inclined--however, they do not *have to*. Above all, their actions are governed by what Great Spirit will allow.

TOTEMIC ANIMALS

According to the Elders, each totemic animal was a special manito.

Basil Johnston wrote that the satisfaction of the human being's basic needs was traditionally met through societal units symbolized by totems which in turn symbol-ized the "incorporeal beings" who assisted the first humans long ago.[15]

The Elders told stories about a time in the very distant past when these special manitos, while still on the Earth in physical body forms, united biologically with humans to form the various totemic clans of traditional human societies.

SUPREME EVIL SPIRIT ?

The Elders explained that the concept of a supreme evil spirit, similar to the

European concept of the Devil, is a European-introduced concept. The native peoples believed in the existence of negative evil forces; however, these were usually counterbalanced by the coexisting positive forces of the universe. Both emanated from the same source, the Great Spirit, who is amoral and contains both positive and negative forces within. Normally these forces existed in a balanced condition; nevertheless, Now-World beings can, and often do, perform acts which bring about imbalance for varying lengths of time.

There is a concept of a being who is sometimes referred to as "Matchi Manitou," who is thought of as very evil. This concept, however, appears to have developed as a result of Christian influence on American Indian philosophy.

UNDERWATER MANITOS

The Elders described these manitos as sometimes manifesting in the form of horned, lion-like underwater beings. It was believed that these beings possessed great "power" potential and could be quite dangerous. They brought about very stormy water conditions that could injure or even kill humans that happened to be on the waters at the time.

Tribal peoples sometimes made herbal offerings to underwater manitos in hopes of assuring good fishing.

Not long ago, an American Indian from one of the Wisconsin reservations told me that some of the Elders believed that recent drownings on the reservation were caused by underwater beings who are displeased with developments there.

MISSHIPESHU

One of the most powerful manitos tied to negative power is Misshipeshu. This being is sometimes seen in the form of a huge horned cat.

Some of the Elders cautioned that one should not even say the name of this being without taking certain ritual precautions so as not to invoke or invite Misshipeshu to come to the human who said the name. Unless the human was trained and prepared to deal with Misshipeshu's presence, grave danger was possible.

WINDIGO

Whether or not the Windigo is an Atisokanak entity is uncertain. The stories told about it are possibly interwoven with recollections of a long-extinct Now-World being. On the other hand, the Windigo may have always been thought of as a manito.

Various Elders considered the Windigo to be allied with great negative forces. Manifesting most often at the coldest times of the winter months, it was sometimes referred to as "The Great Ice and Snow Monster." The Elders also taught that sometimes the Windigo did indeed possess its human victims.

Some scholars have gone to great lengths to associate the Windigo phenomenon with practice of cannibalism by claiming that the tribal peoples believed that the Windigo turned humans into cannibals by starving them. Statements about cannibalism are controversial at best. Although ritual cannibalism may have been practiced at times in many parts of the world, including North America, evidence of the practice is often difficult to authenticate.

I cite Lynne G. Goldstein, a highly respected archaeologist and expert on Aztalan, the ancient settlement site in southern Wisconsin where cannibalism is alleged to have been practiced. This is what Goldstein wrote about "the presumed cannibalism" at Aztalan:

> The only evidence for cannibalism at Aztalan is that some broken human bones were found in refuse pits....[T]here is a great deal of misunderstanding and oversimplification about what these bones might mean....[M]any societies process the bodies of their dead...some parts may be curated or kept for years before burial, while other parts are discarded...a common practice...well documented for both Late Woodland and Mississippian societies....[T]here is no clear evidence of cannibalism at Aztalan.[16]

Many of the scholars who write about cannibalism among American Indian peoples provide very little solid evidence. Linking the Windigo to cannibalism may be a misguided attempt to account for the similarity between descriptions and narratives of the Windigo phenomenon and those of European vampirism and lycanthropy (werewolf phenomenon). The similarities are striking. The uncertainty as to whether or not the Windigo was actually a real being who possessed its victims lends an aura of mystery, horror, and fascination to the Windigo which is similar to its European counterparts.

NOTES

1. A. Irving Hallowell, "Ojibwa Ontology, Behavior, and World View," *Teachings From The American Earth: Indian Religion and Philosophy*, eds. Dennis and Barbara Tedlock, (New York: Liveright, 1975), 150.

2. Basil Johnston, *Ojibway Language Lexicon*, (Toronto: Department of Ethnology, Royal Ontario Museum, 1978), 24.

3. Louis Hennepin, *A Description of Louisiana*, trans. John G. Shea, (1880; n.p.,1966), 333.

4. Andrew J. Blackbird, *History of the Ottawa and Chippewa Indians of Michigan...and Personal and Family History of the Author*, (Ypsilanti, Michigan: Ypsilantian Job Printing House, 1887), 14.

5. John C. Wright, *The Crooked Tree: Indian Legends of Northern Michigan*, (Harbor Springs, Michigan: M.A. Erwin, 1917), 26-27.

6. John M. Cooper, *The Northern Algonquian Supreme Being*, The Catholic University of America Anthropological Ser. 2, (Washington, D.C.: Catholic University of America, 1934), 37.

7. Ibid, 39. My emphasis.

8. Louise Phelps Kellogg, ed., *Early Narratives of the Northwest 1634-1639*, (New York: n.p., 1917), 111.

9. Cooper, 39.

10. Gustaf Stromberg, *The Soul of the Universe*, (Philadelphia: David McKay and Co., 1940), 211-233.

11. Gustaf Stromberg, "The Searchers," *Science of Mind*, (1967).

12. R. R. Baraga, *A Dictionary of the Otchipwe Language,* (1878; Minneapolis: Ross & Haines, Inc., 1973), 114, 238.

13. Johnston, *Lexicon,* 24. My emphasis.

14. Keewaydinoquay, *Directions We Know: Walk In Honor*, (1979), 14-15.

15. Basil Johnston, *Ojibway Heritage*, (1976; University of Nebraska Press, 1990), 61.

16. R. E. Ritzenthaler, *Prehistoric Indians of Wisconsin*, revised by Lynne G. Goldstein, (Milwaukee: Milwaukee Public Museum, 1985), 61-63.

CHAPTER THREE
CREATION AND THE "EARLY EARTH WORLD"

There are several versions of the creation story known to American Indians of the Great Lakes region. In many of these versions the universe begins when Great Spirit starts dreaming and then manifests into 'being' everything within the dream.

The Elders taught that all creation is the act of the One Great Spirit, although Great Spirit utilized other created beings to help with specific aspects of the ongoing process of creation. The Atisokanak World beings called the *Ashkibewig*, whose name actually translates as "Helpers," often act as special assistants to Great Spirit during this process.

According to the Elders, the first things Great Spirit dreamt of and then brought forth into 'being' were the four primary elements: fire, air, water, and earth.

After creating the planet Earth, Great Spirit positioned her in such a manner so that the Sun (*Geezis*) and the Moon (*Tibi-geezis* or "Night Sun") would take turns watching over Earth Mother and her creatures.

Humans were created last and were given comparatively weak physical powers; however, as Basil Johnston points out, humans were given "the greatest gift--the power to dream."[1]

The following story, which takes place at the time of the creation of the Earth, is based on one told by several Elders, including Keewaydinoquay, an educator, herbalist, and medicine woman from the Leelanau and Beaver Islands area of Michigan.[2]

The Bird-People were the last Earth creatures manifested into being before the creation of the humans.

Before the Bird-People were completely finished, Great Spirit became so busy that Great Spirit said to the Sun Spirits, "Now these winged ones who fly through the air should be beautiful, but I will leave you to decide how they will look." So the Sun Spirits went to work at this task.

Now because the Sun encompasses all colors, the Sun Spirits decided to color the Bird-People in a similar manner. Some of the Bird-People were colored like the sunrise, some were colored like the sunset, some were like high noon--colored bright white--for that is what you get when all the colors are mixed together. The

Sun Spirits also splashed some of the Bird-People with leaves, and some with water and some with earth. This is why there are birds of every color and there are others with splashes of many different colors, too.

The Sun Spirits then asked Great Spirit to take a look at the work they had done. Great Spirit looked about and saw all of these wonderfully colored winged-ones running and jumping and hopping and flying and singing everywhere. It was such an absolutely joyous sight that Great Spirit began to laugh a tremendous, long, loud, joyous laugh. The laughter rolled across the waters, and echoed among the hills, reverberated amongst the clouds, and even vibrated into the Spirit World where the Spirit Helpers were so happy that they also laughed their own kind of laugh.

There was one thing, though, that the Spirit Helpers had forgotten while they were laughing. This was a "creating moment" and everything that happened during such a moment came into being. Consequently, when the great, long, loud laugh rang out, it was put into Earth space and into Earth time. The laughter was manifested into being!

Great Spirit was about to zip off to take care of other universal business when the Sun Spirits said, "Great Spirit, please excuse us, but, well, the sound that has been made by the laughter--it now exists in time and space. Doesn't the sound have to have some form so that it won't go bouncing all over the Earth making every creature crazy from listening to it all of the time?"

"All right," Great Spirit replied. "Do that. Put a body on it. I would really like the creatures of Earth to hear the laughter of creation--but not all the time so they go crazy from it. Find something to use as the body for the laughter."

Because it was already early evening on the day of the creation of the Bird-People, about the only thing that the Sun Spirits saw when they looked down upon the Earth were shadows. The Sun Spirits said, "Shadows! You will be the body for that sound." With that, the shadows became the body for the laughter of creation.

Now then, here was this pitiful grayish-black shape, with no colors--no colors at all! Here was just this grayish-black thing, the last of the winged-ones to be created, made from shadows; this was the embodiment of the laughter of creation. All that night, this shadowy winged-one rode quietly on the waters, not knowing who she or he was, or why she or he was brought forth, nor what she or he was supposed to do--knowing only that she or he existed. So, not having anything else to do, this last-created winged-one simply waited patiently.

(The Elders said that this reminds us that we must be patient and trust in Great Spirit's plans for us.)

Back then, in that ancient time, no one knew exactly why Great Spirit had been so busy and didn't visit Earth for many days; but now we know why. It was because Great Spirit was meeting with the Star People and the Atisokanak People regarding the plans for creating the first humans on the Earth.

Meanwhile, as several days passed and the first rays of the Sun touched the waters, the Sun Spirits sensed that the shadowy creature was in distress.

Sure enough. The Shadowy One's eyes were not gray and dull as they greeted the rising Sun, instead, they were red with distress.

But suddenly--as the warmth of the Sun's rays flitted across the grayish black form--OUT came the wondrous sound of the laughter of creation. This sound bounced across the waters, lingered along the shore, and echoed in the hills. All the other creatures on the earth stopped and listened to the joyous sound that seemed to come from the shadows.

Many more days went by, and all the winged-ones flew, and swooped, and dived, and swam, and sang, and soared, and did all sorts of interesting things--all except one, the shadowy grayish-black one, who was still floating on the waters, waiting to know who she or he was, and why she or he was created, and what she or he was supposed to do.

At last Great Spirit completed plans for the creation of the human beings. With the help of the Star People, the first humans were placed on the Earth. Great Spirit told the humans that the Earth was their mother and that she and her other children would teach them the deep secrets of life so that they would always live in balance. Great Spirit also told the humans that the animals and birds were their sisters and brothers along the path of the Sun Trail.

Now, the humans were so new at this business of living that they didn't quite understand what it all meant. But the others who were created earlier understood, and they said they would help this newest creature, even though it seemed that everyone had their own opinion about relative merits of the humans. The animals all agreed that, since Great Spirit was Creator, these human beings must be a part of some greater plan within the natural order of the universe.

Once the humans began to walk and run, the animals and birds would accompany them. They talked with them too. All of the animals had by this time taught the humans something--that is, all of the animals except the dog and the little shadowy grayish-black one. (Much more will be said about Dog and Dog's very special role later.)

Meanwhile the strange, little, bewildered Shadowy One was still waiting on the waters, wondering. Shadowy One did not offer to teach the humans anything because Shadowy One only knew how to do one thing, and that was how to go under the water. Shadowy One couldn't see as how the humans would be interested in that! So Shadowy One simply watched and waited...and waited...and waited....

Then Shadowy One saw Sea-gull soaring on the offshore winds. It looked like a wonderfully exciting thing to do! Shadowy One, not knowing any better, and looking really funny at first, tried to soar too. The winds caught Shadowy One and carried the grayish-black shape up very high, then let go so that down the poor creature went--kersplash!--right into the water. After a few tries though, Shadowy

One got pretty good at landing and never really minded the splashing at all.

Soon Kingfisher, who had been waiting and watching poised on a branch over the water, dove right into the water and--swoosh!--caught a fish. Shadowy One thought, "So that is how Kingfisher gets food--by diving and swimming under the water. Well, maybe I can do that too." Shadowy One tried, and found that it wasn't hard to do at all.

Now, it so happened that on one of these dives, Shadowy One bobbled up near the foot of a high rock where a male human being sat looking down.

By this time the humans had learned many things from the animals. Each time the humans learned something new, the animals would cheer them on with a kind of woodland hurrah, and soon, by way of this encouragement, the humans got to thinking that there wasn't anything in the whole world that they couldn't learn to do. When the human saw that the little Shadowy One could go under the water, on top of the water, and through the air, he said to himself, "If that Shadowy One can fly, then I can fly. If that Shadowy One can swim under the water, then I can swim under the water too. For I am human--the *Wondrous One*."

When the Water Spirits saw the human spread his arms to fly, they called, "No! No!" But the human didn't listen and went right off the cliff! Down, down into the clear, cold water he went with his long black hair streaking behind him.

Now deep in that water there were a lot of sunken logs filled with branches, and waiting nearby there were many Spirits who had overheard the human's proud thoughts. These Spirits did not like the human's superior attitude at all, so they reached out and snagged his long hair on the branches of the sunken logs. As he struggled to free himself, the Spirits just tied more knots in his hair. Many of the animals and birds shrieked their danger calls and rushed to the cliff to watch the struggling human still caught deep in the water. The fishes tried to free him, but they could not. Many of the other animals tried, but they could not. Either they couldn't dive, or they couldn't hold their breath long enough, or whatever-- nobody could free the human from the tangle.

The animals realized that they were about to lose the human. They shouted, "Isn't there *anyone* who can fly through the air, and swim under water, and stay down there long enough to free the human's hair?"

Up swam the little Shadowy One, saying "I have experience at all those things. I'll try. I can use my beak to cut his hair and free him." With that, Shadowy One dove into the depths of the water and tried to cut the knotted hair, but the human fought against the poor creature. Again the Spirits overheard the human's thoughts, "My long black hair is my most handsome feature and I'll not part with it!"

What could little Shadowy One do? Patiently, the poor creature began to untangle the hair, strand by strand. When it became obvious that the human could not hold his breath any longer, Shadowy One went to the surface, gulped as much air as possible, then dove down again, and with it's beak inside the human's mouth, Shadowy One forced air into the human's lungs. Finally, Shadowy One freed the human, and the human rose to the surface of the water, gasping. The top-of-the-water animals pushed him to the shore where he finally stood on his wobbly legs.

One would think that the human would be very grateful indeed. But this human was arrogant, and he just turned and bowed as though he had been the hero of the entire affair!

The animals were amazed by this. They told him that he should be grateful and that he ought to reward the strange little Shadowy One who had rescued him. The human was annoyed with the suggestion that he was obliged to anyone. He tossed his hair in the wind and said, "I don't know why I should. That Shadowy One didn't have to come down there if he didn't want to. Besides, I am human; I deserve to be saved. I am obliged to no earth creature--let alone a little grayish-black shadowy one who doesn't even know who he is!"

The animals became angry then, remembering how they had taught everything they knew to this arrogant human being. They turned to the little Shadowy One and said, "You put your life in danger for him and he doesn't even appreciate it. As for us, we shall rarely trust these humans again. Don't you think we should help you get even with him? We ought to pick his eyes out or cut off his toes when he's swimming."

But the little, grayish-black Shadowy One, who was very tired, just sat in a huddle on a rock, feeling sick at heart and quite miserable, whispering, "No...no...no."

Now the Sun Spirits had seen everything--as they always do. The arrogant human had gone off without even thanking the Shadowy One, and the Sun Spirits were angry about it. The Sun Spirits said, "There is something we will do. We should have done it before, but we kept putting it off waiting for Great Spirit to do it. You deserve a real name because are *mahng.*"

Now "mahng" means "brave," and when the Sun Spirits called Shadowy One "mahng," they had just meant to compliment the creature, but Shadowy One, thinking that Mahng was its new name, burst into the strange and joyous call--*the sound of the laughter of creation!*

After that, the Sun Spirits did not have the heart to change the name. To this day, all animals and birds stop at the twilight to hear Mahng's call, which is the laughter of creation. They nod their heads wisely and say, "Mahng is a good name for the Shadowy One; no other is truly as brave."

Noticing that almost all of creation paused and listened in the twilight and also at dawn to Mahng's call, the Sun Spirits said, "Oh, Mahng, you deserve every color there is to wear, but we cannot give you any colors because we already gave them to the other winged-ones. But, there is something we can do; we can place dabs of shining light upon your feathers."

So all around the grayish-black neck, and down across the dark breast, the Sun

Spirits put dabs of shining light on each feather.

That is why, to this day, *the Loon* wears a shining necklace; to show how brave it had been while patiently waiting for Great Spirit to reveal the special reason for creating Shadowy One so long ago. And that is why, to this very day, the Anishinabeg Western Great Lakes American Indian word for "brave" and for "loon" is the same, "mahng."

At every sunrise and at twilight in the natural places of the northern part of the Western Great Lakes region, Mahng continues to remind all of creation that the laughter of Great Spirit and the Spirit Helpers rang out across the waters when the Earth was new.

There is much that one can learn about a culture by knowing its creation-related stories. The foregoing story, which recounts the origin of the loon's strange and other-worldly call, stresses the importance of not judging anything, or anyone, simply upon appearances. That the shadows, in an almost off-handed way, would become the embodiment of the divine laughter of Great Spirit and the Spirit Helpers is a reminder that even the most lowly forms may have an important role to play in the plans of the Great Spirit. For a human being not to recognize that other beings in the universe deserve the same respect, regardless of their perceived shortcomings, denies an essential truth of creation: the joy of the Great Spirit in bringing forth *all* beings. This, incidentally, shows us how laughter and joy are an integral part of the process of creation. The call of the loon and even our own laughter and joy remind us of the complete delight not expressible in words that the Great Spirit experiences in the continual bringing forth of all things into existence. Because Great Spirit brings all creatures into 'being' with great joy, failing to realize this is a failure to understand the interconnectedness of all aspects of creation. It is a failure to live in balance. The consequences of such actions can be seen in the following story, told by some of the Elders, which picks up where the first story leaves off.

Following the creation of the Earth, a number of colossal changes occurred.

Great Spirit grew extremely unhappy with how the first humans living on Earth were behaving. Most of the humans had drifted away from living lives centered in balance. They were misusing the knowledge that they had been given from the Atisokanak World and from the Star People of other more advanced Now-Worlds. With that knowledge, humans developed technology which far exceeded their ability to use it in a balanced manner. Through the misuse of this technology, they set forces in motion which they had neither the knowledge nor the power to control or reverse. Some of the Earth's land masses literally began to break apart. Great Spirit decided not to intervene to save the human's world because it was in such an advanced state of imbalance.

Then, an onrushing "bearded star" (a comet) plunged into Earth's atmosphere. After breaking into several large sections, many pieces of the bearded star struck the land masses then in the area of the mid-Atlantic, from east of the Yucatan to east of Brazil. That area was the very heart of the human's out-of-balance world. The land masses, which had already begun to break up because of the misuse of technology, now began to sink beneath the waves of the mighty ocean.

Great clouds formed in the sky and a torrential rain fell upon much of the Earth. Even many of the mountains were covered with the water. All that was left of the human's once powerful, developed area was one vast sea with, later, several comparatively small islands. Almost all of the human beings died as unrelenting winds churned the vast stretch of water into a seething mass of waves.

Finally, the rains stopped and the sun appeared. The few human survivors at once began to rebuild their lives in a way that honored Great Spirit and demonstrated their gratitude for saving them. Once again, humans would attempt to live in balance and with respect for everything Great Spirit had created with such joy.

There is a version of an almost Earth-wide flood in most human traditions. This and other American Indian versions of the Great Flood predate the coming of Europeans to the American continents by thousands of years. All of the versions from all traditions appear originally to date from sometime between 10,000 and 9,000 B.C.

NOTES

1. Johnston, *Ojibway Heritage*, 13.

2. "Brave is Mahng is Loon." Keewaydinoquay's version of this story was personally given to me in 1983 along with her "permission to use it in teaching the teachings of the ancestors."

CHAPTER FOUR
THE EARTH AND ITS "PEOPLE"

Chapters two and three focused on the multidimensional world of pure energy which includes the Atisokanak World and its "persons." Now we will examine the worlds where energy is intermixed with matter: the Now-Worlds.

Earth is only one of many Now-Worlds. Other Now-Worlds include the planets in our star system and those in other star systems.

When the Elders used the word "people," they included many physical forms which most individuals from the present European-American society think of as "things"; for instance, Bird-People, Animal-People, and Plant-People, as well as meteorological form "people" (such as Cloud-People), and geological form "people" (such as Rock-People).

Great Spirit manifested all of these Now-World People, including humans, with the inherent responsibility to seek 'balance' and to treat all other beings with honor and respect while functioning as the integral parts of the created universe.

While for the most part all "persons" that Great Spirit created are inherently equal, there are some exceptions. One of the exceptions should be obvious to anybody who has read the previous chapters: the Atisokanak Persons are innately superior to Now-World Persons. The other exception involves what is called the "Primacy of Females," which will be the focus of the last chapter. Despite these exceptions, the belief in the inherent equality of all of creation is essential to Western Great Lakes American Indian metaphysics and establishes the importance of living in 'balance' within one's environment. Treating all aspects of the Now-World environment equally and with great care also underlies another element of Western Great Lakes American Indian metaphysics which Basil Johnston calls the "principle of equal entitlement."[1]

THE PRINCIPLE OF EQUAL ENTITLEMENT

Basil Johnston states that this principle precludes private ownership of the resources of Earth. All created forms, including the unborn, are entitled to the natural benefits of the Earth. During one's lifetime, one is only a trustee of a small portion of the Earth and is required to pass on to future generations the portion inherited from the previous generation. Not only is one to pass it on, but one must also be sure that their portion is in as good of shape, if not better, than when one first became the trustee.

It is important to understand the philosophical significance of this principle in light of the dilemma American Indians confronted when coerced into ''signing'' treaties involving the transfer and assignment of land. What kind of value were they to place on such treaties when they believed that land could not be owned?

> No man can own his mother. This principle extends even to the future. The unborn are entitled to the largesse of the Earth...during life a man [woman] is but a trustee of his [her] portion of the land and must pass on to his [her] children what he [she] inherited from his [her] mother. At death...[one is to take] nothing with them but a memory and [leave] a place for others still to come...no man [woman] can possess his [her] mother; no man [woman] can own the Earth.[2]

The importance of the principle of equal entitlement to the philosophical beliefs and the related religious practices of the Western Great Lakes American Indians serves to further emphasize the connectedness and universal accessibility of Earth to all life-forms. The metaphor of the Earth as Mother, fundamental to the belief system of Western Great Lakes American Indians, enables those who accept the ''ways of the Elders'' to behave and interact with the Earth in the same respectful manner they were taught to treat their own human mothers.

THE FOUR PRIMARY NOW-WORLD ELEMENTS

Through story and example the Elders constantly emphasized the necessity for 'balance' in one's interactions with all of the elements of a Now-World. This was particularly true of the four primary elements, fire, water, air, and earth, into each of which Great Spirit breathed a unique Soul-Spirit.

Under most conditions and circumstances, fire is always first in order of importance. Benton-Banai wrote, ''Every time you use fire you should remember that this is the same fire with which the Creator made the Sun [and] put at the heart of your Mother Earth....[U]se this fire to communicate with the Creator....[U]se it to burn tobacco and let its smoke carry your prayers to Gitchi Manitou.''[3] The Elders taught that fire is a very special gift from Great Spirit and that one is always to respect and take proper care of this gift. Fire has many positive qualities which are beneficial to humans; however, like other natural forces, because of the amoral and dual nature of the universe, it also contains the potential to cause great harm. If one neglects fire, or uses it in an incorrect or unbalanced way, it can injure and destroy.

As with fire, the Elders taught that it is important to use the other three primary elements, earth (i.e. the natural products of Mother Earth such as soil, rock, etc.), water, and air, in a balanced manner. Since they too are subject to the amoral and dual nature of the universe, each element has the potential to manifest itself in either a positive or negative manner. Water, for example, is life-sustaining when it quenches one's thirst or irrigates forests and crops, but it can also drown one. Air is necessary for most life, but within air are forces such as storms which may cause injury or death. The products of the earth; for instance minerals like uranium, may be very beneficial, but they may also be terribly destructive, depending upon how they are used. Again the stress is on learning to consider the consequences of one's actions in the Now-World, and understanding how these actions may be interconnected with the existence of other Now-World People. With this in mind, let the Elders' reminder to "walk and act in balance" be your guide.

THE FOUR WINDS

The Elders taught that the Four Winds are a type of Now-World People--not the inanimate forces they are considered to be in contemporary Western culture. Because they are "people," each wind has a personal name:

East Wind	"Wabanodin" or "Waubininodin"
South Wind	"Shawanodin" or "Zhawaninodin"
West Wind	"Ningaabinodin"
North Wind	"Keewaedinodin" or "Giiwedinodin"

The Elders taught that the Wind Persons are responsible, under the direction and allowance of certain Atisokanak Persons, for changes in seasons and weather. Because tribal peoples were so often dependent upon the actions of the winds, they designed rituals to attempt in a balanced manner to influence the Wind Persons.

GRANDFATHER ROCK

The Elders said that the rock is a symbol of the unchanging Atisokanak World in a Now-World of almost constant change.

They talked of a rather widespread American Indian custom of using certain rocks and rock formations as transformers and substations for Atisokanak-based "power."

In the Western Great Lakes area there are several places the Elders knew of where such rocks and formations exist. One of these is located in Sheboygan County in southeastern Wisconsin, where Pyawasit said a very large crystal buried deep in a prominent hill creates an energy vortex causing unusual manifestations. Some individuals claim to have seen what they describe as a starship hovering over the hill while an alien-like crew made repairs to the exterior of the craft.

In Ozaukee County, also in southeastern Wisconsin, there is a large rock which looks like the Egyptian god of light, Horus-Ra. This rock intermittently appears to cause compass variations.

In each location, there is another large rock which appears to have some kind of unexplainable healing ability. Pyawasit said that at one time there were American Indian villages at both locations because of these unique healing rocks.

Many tribal Elders pointed out that all stones and rocks are, or have been at one time, living persons who can communicate. The problem is that there are very few humans who listen. The living Rock-People can feel, can see you, and are waiting to teach the sincere. In the old days, when hunters or others lost their way, they knew that if they asked the rocks or stones in a sincere manner they would be pointed in the proper direction.

Pyawasit emphasized that certain rocks and stones must sometimes be fed. As an example, while in the Lake Tomahawk area of north-central Wisconsin during a field session, he pointed out a very large rock to a group of university students studying aspects of American Indian culture. He took great care to show the students that this particular rock had eyes and ears, a nose, and a mouth. He showed them that the traditional way of feeding the rock was to put some tobacco at the mouth. Some of the students were later heard, away from Pyawasit's hearing, scoffing at the ridiculousness of what he had told them. Amazingly, those particular students could not find the rock the next day--even after making every effort to find it! Other students found it and pointed it out to those who had not believed Pyawasit; but the skeptical students said that they still could not see the rock even though it was right before their eyes. Pyawasit said that the Rock-Person was hiding from them. As unbelievable as this incident may seem, there were several witnesses (including visiting faculty members from the University of Wisconsin system) who at the time agreed that they had seen this phenomenon. Regrettably, most would later deny that they had been witness to it. This later denial, perhaps, is a human sanity protective mechanism at work.

PLANT-PEOPLE AND HUMAN/PLANT RELATIONSHIPS

Great Spirit created the Plant-People long before creating the Animal-People, and even longer before placing the first human beings on Earth. As a gift from Great Spirit, the Plant-People have the ability to conjoin a portion of their Spirit with the Spirit of both like and unlike species to form a kind of common Spirit in valleys, meadows, bays, hills, and certain other natural places. The moods of the Plant-People reflect the state of being of a particular place. If some of the Plant-People in a given area are destroyed or even negatively altered in some way, it would change the mood of the entire place.

Plant-People do not need animals or humans to exist in their native habitat; however, animals and humans cannot exist without Plant-People since they cannot survive without the oxygen plants produce.

The Elders said that certain rules governing the relationship between human beings and the Plant-People developed over time. The rules are based in large part on observation of the natural world. The special rules governing this relationship include the following:

Take only those plants and only as much of those plants as one really needs. Take only that part of the plant which is needed. One must also learn, and constantly keep in mind, the significant difference between needing and wanting.

Never take all of the plant, or the only plant of its kind in an area. If the plant reproduces by root system, one must leave enough of the root; if the plant reproduces by seed, be sure to scatter some seed. If the plant is not yet mature, leave enough so that it may mature and reproduce. If one is not sure how it reproduces, leave enough of all parts.

Prior to taking any plants or plant parts, make an offering to the Great Spirit and to the Atisokanak Life-Form Master of that species. Explain why you need to take the plant and ask for understanding and forgiveness. Once you take, use all that you take; no waste is allowed!

THE TREE OF LIFE

The *Tree of Life* is thought of as the sacred link connecting the world on Earth with both the Underworld and the world of Air and Sky.

The Tree of Life is the White Cedar tree. She is called "Grandmother Cedar." Significantly, even though she is turned and twisted by the winds, she endures, as humans must learn to endure through adversity.

The Elders would tell the children that, if they were ever separated from their families and became lost in the forest, they should seek out Grandmother Cedar and her companion, Grandfather Birch, because they would provide all that was needed until the lost individual was found.

Grandmother Cedar is also symbolic of 'balance' because the shape and height of the tree-portion above the ground mirrors the root-portion below the ground.

The Elders called Grandfather Birch the "Child of the Thunderers" because he is impervious to lightning strikes.

THE ANIMAL-PEOPLE AND THEIR RELATIONSHIPS WITH HUMANS

After the Earth was almost destroyed by the massive flood, the Animal-People, who had always continued to live in 'balance' (even while the humans had not), assisted the surviving humanoid people in rebuilding the human communities.

Several Elders told a story of a time when many of the animals, who had shown great concern for the welfare of the often relatively helpless humans, became thoroughly disgusted with the humans. Many humans had taken advantage of their relationship with the Animal-People and had become extremely selfish and greedy. Many cared little for the welfare of other life-forms. The animals, led by Bear, held a great meeting to determine what should be done about the negative situation which had developed because of human selfishness. The animals decided to approach Great Spirit and request permission to exterminate the humans. Great Spirit was also pretty disillusioned and fed up with the behavior of the humans. Consequently, Great Spirit gave permission to carry out a plan of action.

As the animals were preparing their attack plan, Dog quietly slipped away and ran to warn the humans! The humans, because they had been warned, were able to prepare for and thwart the animal attack. The other animals were furious and confronted Dog demanding to know the reason why Dog acted in direct opposition to the decisions of the animal council and Great Spirit.

"For a long time," Dog responded, "I observed most of you other animals serving these helpless human beings. I always felt that, at some point in time, I too must contribute something. I wanted to help the humans and I saw that I could save them." The unselfish love and devotion which was necessary for Dog to warn the humans became Dog's gift.

Because Dog betrayed the other animals by choosing to side with the humans, the other animals decided that Dog must somehow be punished. They approached Great Spirit and convinced Great Spirit of their need for justice in this case. Great Spirit declared that Dog was to be thereafter servile to humans, to be subject to the human being's fluctuating moods and whims which sometimes even manifest in cruelty. Since that time, unless a dog is psychologically disturbed, dogs have stayed at the side of humans, demonstrating sincere, continuing love and devotion even when it is not returned.

At that time also, the animals received Great Spirit's permission to change their languages so that most humans would no longer be able to understand them.

As is the case with the Plant-People, the Elders taught that there are special rules which govern the human relationship with the Animal-People. The special rules include the following:

One may hunt and kill animals, including fish, only when there is a real need, bearing in mind that to want and to need are not the same thing. As is the case with the plants, prior to taking animal life, one must make an offering to the Atisokanak Life-Form Master of the particular species and also to Great Spirit, then explain why it is necessary to take the life of the animal and ask for understanding and forgiveness. In addition, female animals of all kinds, including fish, who are in the season of their probable pregnancy are to be spared.

Females who are in the stage of still providing necessary care for their young are also to be spared. The young themselves, cubs, fawns, etc., are to be spared as well. Only one healthy male is necessary for impregnating several females; therefore, male animals are always the preferred choice.

One must use all one takes; no waste is allowed. The remains are to be treated with respect, as one would treat human remains.

IMPORTANCE OF EAGLES

As stated previously, eagles are thought to be very special Now-World Persons. One of their responsibilities is to help convey the petitions of human beings to the Thunderers of the Atisokanak World. The Thunderers in turn relay those petitions to Great Spirit.

The Elders taught that eagles are often messengers of the Atisokanak People. When one sees an eagle circling in the sky, it is a good sign. The Elders described ceremonies and other situations in which individuals reported hearing the sound of great wings beating above them and felt the air whirling past from the powerful beat. Others have reported feeling the grip of strong talons on their arms or hands.

Some scholars have conjectured that these accounts are either the product of minds susceptible to suggestion, or caused by mass hypnosis. The Elders would say that the scholars who propose this simply haven't learned to see, hear, and feel manifestations from the Atisokanak World.

Some of the Elders told a story about an ancient time when Great Spirit was so very angry with the behavior of the humans that Great Spirit almost exterminated them. According to the story, Eagle approached Great Spirit out of compassion for the human beings and asked if Great Spirit would spare them if there were at least one community of humans still endeavoring to live in appropriate 'balance'. Great Spirit agreed. The Elders said that since that time, each day a great eagle flies from east to west over the land observing all of humankind. As long as Eagle is able to report finding one community of humans truly trying to live in 'balance', Great Spirit refrains from exterminating the humans. The Elders cautioned that this is one of the many reasons why humans are not to take the life of Eagle-People.

BEAR IS ALSO VERY SPECIAL

The Elders told a story which involved many beings, including Bear, who at one time in the distant past had humanoid forms and lived below the surface of the Earth. According to the story, long, long ago a special Manito Council was held for the purpose of trying to assist a strange new type of Now-World being called a "human." It was decided at the council that, in order to assist these seemingly helpless and fragile beings, an effective channel of communication linking the Below-the-Earth Creatures with the Above-the-Earth Creatures needed to be established. The council chose the Life-Form Masters of the Otter and the Bear to have primary responsibility for the task. They in turn instructed an especially chosen otter and bear who lived below the surface of the earth to do the actual physical work. Bear pushed up the first Tree of Life (the Cedar tree) from below the surface of the earth while Otter pulled and guided the tree from above. Finally, after a great deal of strenuous effort, the Tree of Life emerged into the sunlight, followed by Bear. Otter was anxious to return with Bear to their below-the-surface world, but Bear wanted to look around and began curiously sniffing the warm smells of the surface world. Then Bear, feeling even still more inquisitive, wanted to take a good look at these human creatures to see what was so special about them that the Manito Council should request so much effort be expended on their behalf. Bear did not have far to look. They came upon a group of the humans who, upon seeing Bear and Otter, fled in fright. They all ran and hid except for a small child who could not even stand. Bear stared at the unfortunate creature and commented to Otter that it was no wonder they needed help so badly, they didn't even have claws, or fangs, or much fur at all!

Meanwhile as the warm sun shone upon the Cedar, Otter slipped away into the refreshing surface-world waters where Otter continues to play to this day--unless threatened by the descendants of the first human beings. Bear also stayed in the surface-world but always returns each late autumn or early winter to a cave or other extension of the world below the surface to sleep and wait throughout the long, cold winter until the warm smells of spring fill the air in the world above. Since that time, so very long ago, other Animal-People from the below-the-surface world have also come to live above the surface, and following the example of Bear and Otter, they also significantly assisted the humans.

Upon seeing a bear, respectful humans will address it as "Grandfather" or "Grandmother" in recognition of the bear's important role in establishing the Tree of Life as a channel of communication between the two worlds above and below the surface of the earth.

In addition, bear bones are treated with a special ceremonial reverence. Quite a number of years ago, a bear skull was found on an island located between Michigan's Upper and Lower Peninsulas. The person who found it realized that this was quite unusual because the island is located a considerable distance from any mainland areas where bears usually live. The person took the skull to a large city in another state, planning to have it scientifically analyzed.

The person later reported that he had experienced a series of intense personal troubles since taking the skull from the island. An American Indian Elder advised the person to return the skull to the place where he had found it. The person took the Elder's advice and soon after reported that the troublesome episodes had ended.

According to several American Indian Elders, the island where the skull was found had been known at one time throughout the Western Great Lakes area as "Bear Medicine Island." There is an old ceremonial area on this particular island which is called the Bear Circle.

The Menominee also have special stories about a great white bear who is said to have emerged from a cave at Minikani, near the mouth of the Menominee River where it enters Green Bay. Some versions of these stories suggest that the Menominee people are descendants of some kind of union between the white bear and one of the earlier humans.

MEDICINE SNAKES

The Medicine Island in Michigan is at times inundated with snakes, both in the waters along the shoreline and on the land. They normally do not harm humans; nonetheless, their very presence tends to ward off any unwelcome visitors to this very special place.

In many of the tribal groups, the snake is a medicine symbol of healing and renewal.

THE FOUR HILLS OF LIFE

The Elders taught about the various stages of life by comparing them to hills which one has to climb one after the other.[4]

At birth one faces the first hill and continues to climb it throughout infancy. At the first hill, one is the embodiment of 'centered' potential that should be fulfilled by living in 'balance' in accordance with Great Spirit's design.

As one begins to climb the second hill during the time of youth and adolescence, the human begins to "bloom" in both spiritual and physical power. It is while on this hill that young males between the ages of twelve and fourteen are expected to initiate contact with the Atisokanak World through the solitary quest for a Vision.

The third hill is reached in adulthood and often includes parenthood. As one climbs this hill one usually faces many burdens, duties, responsibilities, and uncertainties. It is at this time that one may encounter psychological and spiritual detours on one's life path. The Elders said the Atisokanak People will allow one to digress from a balanced life path. Nevertheless, after each digression, the traveler must return to the proper balanced path without betraying any established trust relationships with the positive entities of the Atisokanak World. If the traveler does lose the way and digresses, he or she must find his or her own way back since only the traveler knows where he or she departed from the true path in the first place. The Elders are available to advise and counsel, but all travelers must take the corrective action on their own. If one does not return to the path of 'balance', or if one betrays an Atisokanak trust, the individual's Soul will have to reincarnate in order to correct and then enhance the 'balance' which had been upset at the point of digression in the previous lifetime.

The climb up the fourth hill occurs in what is called old age--a relative term. At this time one notices a lessening of strength and endurance and a waning of agility. According to the Elders, the mere fact of being alive to climb this fourth hill should be thought of as a gift from Great Spirit. While one is climbing the last of the Four Hills, one has the responsibility of passing on all accumulated positive wisdom to those who are following behind on the first three hills.

There are many versions of an ancient ceremony for newborn infants which ritually reinforces the symbolism of the Four Hills of Life. Here is a version of a prayer

typically used in this ceremony. The ceremonial leader begins praying while holding
the infant and facing East:

Ho! Sun, Moon, Stars, all you that move in the heavens,
  I bid you hear me!
Into your midst has come a new life!
  Help make smooth its path that it may reach the crest of the First Hill!
Ho! Winds, Clouds, Rain, Mist, all you that move in the air,
  I bid you hear me!
Into your midst has come a new life!
  Help make smooth its path that it may reach the crest of the Second Hill!
Ho! Hills, Valleys, Rivers, Lakes, Trees, Grasses, all you of the Earth,
  I bid you hear me!
Into your midst has come a new life!
  Help make smooth its path that it may reach the crest of the Third Hill!
Ho! Birds great and small that fly in the air,
Ho! Animals great and small that dwell in the forest,
Ho! Insects that fly and creep among the grasses and burrow in the ground,
  I bid you hear me!
Into your midst has come a new life!
  Help make its path smooth that it may reach the crest of the Fourth Hill!
Ho! All you of the Heavens, All you of the Air, All you of the Earth:
  I bid you all to hear me!
Into your midst has come a new life!
  *Help make its path smooth that it may travel, in balance, beyond the Four
Hills!*[5]

THE IMPORTANCE OF THE INITIAL NAMING

The Elders explained that the initial naming of an individual is crucially important
because, prior to receiving a name, the individual is mostly potential waiting to be
fulfilled. Through the act of naming, the individual receives his or her identity from
the Atisokanak World.

The *Initial Name* is itself a gift to the human from the Atisokanak World which the
Namer, usually a respected Elder, obtains from the Atisokanak World through special
dream-contact with the Atisokanak People.

CENTERING AND BALANCE

Great Spirit incarnates all Now-World Persons into material bodies in a balanced
condition. Their positive potentiality equals their negative potentiality. They are born
centered; that is, in harmony with the Now-World's primal nature.

While still young, often as a result of ignorance, perhaps as a result of arrogance, one begins to travel further and further from one's original, balanced state. This may continue more or less unchecked until some point in life when one begins to wonder what life really means.

To find the answer, one must travel back to the primal balanced state; in other words, one must 'center' the self.

In order to be 'centered' and in 'balance', one must first learn to walk the life path in honor and equilibrium. Along the path it is an obligation to honor those who walked on the path before the individual, as well as to honor those contemporaries who walk alongside. This must be done while at the same time conducting one's self in such a manner as to be remembered with honor by those who will walk this same path long after the individual dies.

None of this can be achieved without the cooperative assistance of the Atisokanak People and the individual's own intense efforts.

DOUBLE VISION

The Elders explained that what they called *double vision* comes from understanding that there are two distinct but related "worlds" of reality: the Now-World and the Atisokanak World. By living in a meaningful relationship to both of them, recognizing aspects of the Atisokanak World in the Now-World, an individual learns to *see* with the Spirit. The place where the two worlds overlap is referred to as the *middle* road of four roads of reality that run side by side. Here, if you are to find your way, you must see with the physical eyes closed and let your spirit-sight be the guide.

DEATH: BELIEFS AND PRACTICES

The Elders taught that the death of the physical body is not the end of the individual. It is instead a transitional step in the ongoing cycle of existence manifested in Great Spirit's spiraling nonlinear space-time continuum.

The Elders stated that the afterworld is located in a dimension of the Atisokanak World. The journey which the Soul and usually the Ghost take to reach the afterworld is a westward journey leading along the path of the Milky Way.

Traditionally, when an individual's Soul was ready to depart for the Atisokanak World, family members and close friends would gather around the dying individual and ritually sing the Soul over to the next cycle of existence. The process of the Soul's preparation and departure for the Atisokanak World is called *westing*.

The interment of the body usually takes place within four days after death since it takes the life-sustaining Soul four days to travel to the Atisokanak World.

During the westing process, the Soul must cross a rapidly flowing river spanned by a log-like, snake-like creature. The Elders said that the Soul must offer this creature the essence of the Kinnikinnick which is customarily placed in the fists of the dead person's body. After the offering is made, the creature would then allow the Soul to cross over the river and continue the westward journey.

The Elders said that an individual's status in the afterworld is corollary to one's positive actions while living in the Now-World. They told stories of how one would enjoy catching large fish in the afterworld if one had sincerely tried to maintain 'balance' in all relationships with other Now-World People and did not abuse any special power relationships with the Atisokanak People. If one had been only mediocre in these relationships, one's chances of catching prize fish in the afterlife were lessened. Negative deeds on the part of Now-World People are dealt with by the Atisokanak People in the Now-World rather than in the afterlife.

Most tribal peoples in the Western Great Lakes area buried the bodies of their dead in the earth. If the ground was frozen, or if for some other reason a body could not be buried right away, they would wrap it in animal hides or blankets and temporarily place it in a tree until it could be properly buried. An exception to this practice involved the Rabbit Clan of some tribal groups. Individuals from this clan cremated rather than buried their dead. They believed that a long and severe winter would result if bodies of this clan were buried in the ground.

Sometimes various items were buried in the grave along with the body. The spirit of these items would then accompany the departing human Soul on the journey to the afterworld. Such items might include familiar and beloved objects selected by the deceased prior to death. The person conducting the burial ceremony would break these objects before putting them in the grave in order to release their spirits so that they may accompany the Soul along the path of the Milky Way.

The Elders said that the dead did not necessarily lose contact with the living but rather took an interest in the affairs of the living, often assisting them, sometimes becoming a nuisance and even causing harm.

The Elders also said that it is definitely possible for the Soul to reincarnate into a different body in any given Now-World; however, there is no possibility of reuniting the Soul with the same body after its death. This, incidentally, does not rule out the possibility of near-death experiences since it is the Ghost portion of the Spirit, not the Soul, which travels to the afterworld in such instances.

There is a story the Elders told about a young couple who were about to be married when the young woman suddenly died before the ceremony had taken place. The young man, grief stricken, was determined to travel to the land of the dead, find his bride-to-be, and return with her to the land of the living. His Elders attempted to dissuade him. They said that living people should not attempt to bring the dead back from the afterworld. Those who have taken the path along the Milky Way should be left to seek the peace of their new home. The Elders continued that it is not good to seek the unattainable; one should let go of an apparently hopeless quest otherwise one's Soul will retain the sorrowful memory long after entering the land of the dead. From each loss one may realize gain. In the case of lost love, it is far better to have known and received love, however short-lived, than never to have known it at all. In one's grief one must remember that for every ending there is a new beginning; just as the trees that shed their leaves in the fall sprout new foliage in spring.

RELIGIOUS PRACTICES

The Elders frequently pointed out that religion is like a golden thread woven through the fabric of life. Consequently, most acts have some religious significance.

They said that religious practices, including prayers, are petitionary, invocatory, and for giving thanks.

The rituals generally followed patterns laid down by ancestors from the various tribes and clans. There is usually not, however, any set formula for prayers. It is instead the sincerity of the human doing the praying which matters more than form. Each prayer should be an expression of the pure and true feeling in one's heart.

Some of the Elders were aware that from the late seventeenth century onward, American Indian religious societies were altered as a result of influence from the Christian missionaries, traders, and government officials who found opportunities to exert pressure on American Indian societies in a state of social and environmental flux. In addition, the Elders acknowledged that contact between tribal groups with whom their ancestors had little, if any, previous contact, would also sometimes bring about significant changes in traditional religious practices. I may add that no religion is static. It would be folly to ignore contemporary American Indian metaphysics on the grounds that it no longer exists in a pure form. A living philosophy can neither be frozen in time nor preserved out of context like the wax exhibits in museums. To do so would be to deny many contemporary American Indians access to their own religious expression since there is not, nor has there ever been, only one right way to express what is in the heart.

THE IMPORTANCE OF DREAMS AND VISIONS

The Elders stated that Dream and Vision experiences are to be thought of as *real* social situations in which the ghost-portion of the Spirit leaves the body of a Now-World Person and travels to the Atisokanak World in order to meaningfully communicate with the Atisokanak People. When the body is in a sleeping state, the experience is a *Dream*. When the body is awake, the experience is said to be a *Vision.*

Dreams are thought of as important educational experiences--a kind of going to school while asleep. Traditionally, children were encouraged to dream, to remember their dreams, and to discuss them with respected Elders.

One is always to take proper precautions in both Dream and Vision situations (as one should in all social situations) because there exists the possibility of negative events occurring. The danger lies in being deceived by a malevolently inclined

Atisokanak Person.

DREAMING WITH INTENT

The Elders said that *dreaming with intent* involves consciously setting out to enter into a specific level of the dream-state in order to make out-of-body contact with an Atisokanak Person or Persons. The purpose of dreaming with intent is to seek and engage the help of the Atisokanak for a specific task or objective.

THE VISION QUEST AND GUARDIAN SPIRITS

The *Vision Quest*, one of the most significant activities which a human *male* would experience during adolescence, is somewhat similar to dreaming with intent. The difference is that the Vision Quest is realized while the body is awake rather than in a state of sleep.

It is usually undertaken at the time of puberty, normally in the young male's twelfth year, and is done with the proper and adequate guidance of knowledgeable Elders. All human males are expected to seek meaningful contact with the Atisokanak World and its beings through the Vision Quest experience. The Vision Quest is particularly important because most human males, unlike females, do not begin life with the ability to conduct Atisokanak "power." Females do not have to undertake a Vision Quest because they are created with an automatic relationship to the Atisokanak. Nonetheless, females can quest for additional knowledge and seek guidance regarding the proper use of the gift. This type of questing is also to be done under proper and adequate guidance of knowledgeable Elders.

During the Vision Quest, an individual may enter into a personal relationship with one or more Atisokanak Persons. Such a relationship would provide the spiritual connection to the Atisokanak World necessary for conducting "power" into a Now-World.

It is also during the Vision Quest that an Atisokanak entity may make itself available to the quester as a *Guardian Spirit*. The Atisokanak Guardian Spirit who chooses to protect and assist an individual can be appealed to, influenced, persuaded, insulted, and alienated just like a human being. Nonetheless, one should be mindful that it is the Atisokanak People, not humans, who have the "power." Carelessness or haughtiness on the part of human beings when dealing with Atisokanak Persons is dangerous!

The Elders said that any number of Atisokanak Persons might choose to appear during the Vision Quest experience. Some individuals received more than one, perhaps several, Atisokanak Guardian Spirits.

For the actual Vision Quest, a youth would be accompanied by his father (or other significant adult male) to a special hierophany and then left there alone. The youth would abstain from food for four days and three nights, taking only life-sustaining fluids such as water or herbal tea as needed. He would be expected to concentrate on initiating meaningful communion with nature and the Atisokanak World.

The parallel between physical hunger and spiritual seeking in the Vision Quest is symbolic of the ontological emptiness at the beginning of the quest. The Atisokanak People are ritually and respectfully asked to fill both voids.

While unobserved, an adult would periodically check on the quester to be sure that he was all right. The adult would not communicate with the quester.

The individual usually returned from the Vision Quest experience with a vivid memory of the event and a special name from the Atisokanak Guardian. A Guardian would also usually give the quester the promise of future help and protection, instructions for making a talisman, and sometimes even a special song for contacting the Guardian.

The talisman, a symbol of the Atisokanak Guardian or Guardians, was often a small leather pouch containing various items which the Atisokanak Person had instructed should be included. These might be small stones, feathers, and other natural items. The talisman would serve as a sort of storage battery for "power" and could be used by the human to call the Guardian or to direct "power" from the Atisokanak World.

During the Vision Quest, the individual might also have received special parapsychological (PSI) abilities as a gift from the Atisokanak World. These may include the ability to facilitate the curing of illnesses and the ability to exercise influence over natural phenomena such as the weather.

Upon returning from the Vision Quest, the youth was also expected to seek out a respected Elder and discuss the entire experience in order to draw upon the Elder's own experiences and wisdom for a better understanding of all that may have transpired. The Elder also provided assistance with the interpretation and understanding of the Vision Quest name.

If one carelessly discussed such an important event as the Vision Quest experience with just anybody, one might inadvertently offend the Atisokanak Guardians, resulting in their becoming disgusted with the individual; consequently, the Guardians would be less likely to intervene on behalf of their human ward in times of need.

There were many variations, both by tribe and clan, to the mechanics of the Vision Quest. The general rule of thumb was that one should do whatever made sense, in terms of safety for the individuals involved, and also considering that one should honor, not offend, the Atisokanak Persons.

The Elders stressed that there are several things to consider when undertaking a Vision Quest. They said that the quester should be careful not to ask for too much too often from the Atisokanak Persons. One should not request to serve as a conduit for more "power" than one is able to control since the result could be threatening to the life and health of not only the individual but also those close to the individual. Again, "power" is amoral and may manifest through Atisokanak Persons who will use it in a negative manner. In addition, the Now-World Persons serving as conduits may be very unpredictable. ''Power'' is potentially dangerous, and is nothing to be played with. Inherently equal Now-World Persons may become, through conduit relationships with Atisokanak Persons of greater hierarchical rank, more ''powerful'' than other Now-World Persons. This is because the intensity of the positive or negative ''power'' that they conduct is also greater.

Also because of this, the Elders would caution one to be careful about who one challenged in the area of shamanism or sorcery lest the individual quickly find himself or herself to be no match for the individual challenged.

The Elders pointed out that some individuals were so excessive in their quests for Atisokanak connections that they became mentally unbalanced and sometimes turned into social outcasts.

In some instances, the Visions that occur during the questing seem to be possibly dangerous or even evil. In those cases the Elders advised that the individual should politely and with respect attempt to decline the relationship with the particular Atisokanak Person or Persons associated with the Vision.

Nonetheless, there are also instances in which the Atisokanak Person (or Persons) compels the quester to accept the relationship since it is the Atisokanak Person who ultimately controls the Vision experience. In such relationships the quester may exhibit symptoms of mental illness, or be responsible for poltergeist activity, or possibly undergo metamorphosis. Sometimes the relationship does not outwardly appear to affect the individual at all.

While the Vision Quest marked the initiation of the relationship necessary for adolescent males to conduct ''power,'' all were advised against aggressively using it at such a young age. Individuals were told that it was best, and safest, to wait until one's hair had begun to turn the color of the snow before actively serving as a conduit. By that time, it was hoped that one would have learned enough to avoid becoming consciously and dangerously foolish with the ability. Those who did not follow this advice often met with negative results.

The individual who establishes contact with the Atisokanak World through the Vision Quest experience is expected to live out and give fulfilling expression to the Vision, which is thought of as a gift to the human from the Atisokanak World. This gift normally comes only to those who are prepared to receive it.

The Elders pointed out that the Vision Quest experience is *not* the only occasion in which Atisokanak Persons might appear to an individual. They usually come when called, as well as arriving unsought when they perceive there is a need to assist and protect an individual with whom they have established a relationship.

ASPECTS OF SHAMANISM

The Elders stated that a shaman is a human being (male or female) who serves as a specialized technician in a ''power'' conduit relationship between the Atisokanak World and a Now-World.

There are some real dangers inherent in this. When one employs any form of energy, be it physical or spiritual energy, there is always the potential hazard of channeling not only positive, but negative "power" into a Now-World. In addition, the personal relationship with the Atisokanak People may become so intimate that the Atisokanak People may possess the shaman. There is also the ever-present danger that an individual may make egotistical use of this other-worldly "power" and walk on the negative side, also sometimes called the "Darkside," of the spectrum of 'balance'. There are many temptations to do this.

Under certain circumstances, the shaman's voice or drum is said to act as a kind of cosmic axis that penetrates into the layers of other dimensions and provides a guideway for the path of "power" leading from the Atisokanak World into the Now-World. The shaman is also sometimes able to lead others across the boundary between the Atisokanak World and a Now-World and then back again.

Because of their role as a conduit of either positive or negative forces, they were among the most feared as well as the most respected individuals of the community.

The shaman can receive his or her calling from an Atisokanak Person at any age, but usually this occurred during puberty.

BEAR WALKERS

As noted in chapter two, *Bear Walkers* are certain shamanistic practitioners capable of metamorphosis into the form of bears and sometimes other animals.

Closely associated with the notion of Bear Walkers are *fireballs*: glowing objects which travel at night along the treetops. Fireballs are either thought to be traveling shamans, or evidence of the practitioner at work.

LOVE SORCERY

With or without the aid of the shaman, *love sorcery* involves using various plant and mineral substances to make an individual physically attractive, perhaps even irresistible, to another. Usually these substances are mixed with a bit of hair from the intended "target." Also called love medicine, the selfish use of love sorcery was thought of as a crime akin to what present society defines as rape.

"WITCHCRAFT"

Some scholars report there is evidence confirming the belief in what *they* term "witchcraft" among the native peoples of the Western Great Lakes region. Most often these reports are about specialized activities and procedures used to harm or even kill others. Some individuals made use of the principles of sympathetic and contagious magic, using effigies (handmade images) of the intended victim in much the same manner used in Caribbean Voudoun (or Voodoo) practices.

Individuals protected themselves from such activities by keeping certain protective objects on their persons which were believed to ward off or neutralize negative sorcery.

RITUAL AND CEREMONY

Most traditional American Indian rituals and ceremonies are ultimately intended to honor Great Spirit. Herbal offerings, music, and dance, in both ceremony and ritual, serve as the medium through which human beings may honor Great Spirit.

In music and in dance, the drumbeat is a heartbeat which symbolically merges the human heartbeat, the heartbeat of Mother Earth, and the heartbeat of all other life-forms in the universe. Rattles and shakers, in addition to drums, echo this universal heartbeat and are thought to attract the attention of the manitos.

Song and dance are to be naturally felt and improvised--not performed according to a plan thought out in advance. The participants should feel themselves become one with all other life-forms in the universe. Ritualistic and ceremonial behavior which is felt, unpremeditated, and therefore most compatible with primal nature, is the most desirable and effective way to honor Great Spirit.

Many songs utilize vocables: human voice sounds imitative of the natural sounds of birds, animals, the winds, and so on. These songs are intended to communicate with Great Spirit and the manitos in the hope of influencing them in some way.

Songs are acquired primarily through Dream and Vision experiences, but they can also be acquired as gifts or through purchase from other individuals.

In many rituals and ceremonies, an herbal mixture of Kinnikinnick is reverently thrown into the air, placed upon earth or water, burned in fire, or smoked in a pipe. Tobacco is a later substitute for Kinnikinnick and the two are often used interchangeably. The Elders stated that Great Spirit created the herbs which make up Kinnikinnick primarily for humans to use in ritual and ceremony. They also said that Great Spirit arranged it so that the only way manitos could get Kinnikinnick was from humans. Manitos like Kinnikinnick and tobacco very much and are appreciative when humans offer it to them.

The Elders taught that it was rare for an individual to take even a pinch of Kinnikinnick or tobacco for any purpose without being aware of an intuitive feeling of reverence for it and for the Atisokanak Persons honored with it. Kinnikinnick is placed with certain objects or in certain locations as offerings to the particular spirit or spirits of those objects and locations. The spirit partakes of the essence--the spiritual element--of the offering. Usually these ritual offerings are confined to keeping spirits in good humor. Kinnikinnick may also be offered in an attempt to calm spirits who are for some reason displeased, or to invoke their active aid. Sometimes an individual will offer the essence of either the Kinnikinnick or tobacco to the spirits by smoking it in a pipe

When ceremonial objects, such as medicine bags, dream bundles, and special spirit stones are put away, a small amount of Kinnikinnick or tobacco is placed with them in hopes that the spirit or spirits associated with these objects will not become dissatisfied and make trouble for the human.

Thunder Stones are special spirit stones which require particular attention. They are round, black stones of various sizes which are somehow related to the lightning-like bolts of energy that the Atisokanak Thunderers occasionally hurl at the Earth.

The individuals who have one or more Thunder Stones in their possession are required to renew the herbal offering kept with the stones four times a year. This must be done upon the occasion of the first peal of thunder in the spring, and again in about the middle of the summer. The Kinnikinnick or tobacco again must be replaced a third time when the thunderstorms cease in fall, and a fourth time during mid-winter.

The Elders said that if the special treatment of a Thunder Stone or any other sacred object were neglected, the Atisokanak Person associated with the particular stone or object might retaliate against the individual who neglected this responsibility. The human must attempt to make sincere reparation as quickly as possible.

The act of reparation might be done in a number of ways. The Elders said that all that may be needed is simply to replace the herbal offering kept with the object, or it might be necessary for the human to give a ceremonial feast during which he or she openly and frankly acknowledges to everyone assembled his or her guilt and negligence in the treatment of the object.

THE CIRCLE

The circle is perhaps the oldest and most universal symbol of Deity. It represents both Creator and created in one and is a reminder of the natural cycles of birth, death, and rebirth in the Now-Worlds.

The Elders stated that the ancient peoples paid particular attention to the circular shape of the Sun and Moon. The ancestors then incorporated that same shape into important aspects of their daily lives including their wigwams (shelters), their ceremonial fires, and their governmental council.

THE COLOR RED

The Elders referred to the color red as the color of life and also of the Morning Star which announces the beginning of each new day from the eastern horizon. Red has special ceremonial significance. It is especially significant to the ceremonies which the Elders said were taught to the humans by the Star People.

THE SEVEN SACRED DIRECTIONS

The Elders *always* discussed the Seven Sacred Directions in the following order, beginning with East and tracing the directions clockwise in a circle:

East, invariably the first of the seven, is the direction of birth and renewal. The Elders said that when a Now-World Person is about to be conceived, a Soul which has not previously experienced an incarnation in a Now-World body is sent from the Atisokanak World into the Now-World to animate the embryo within the mother and sustain life upon its conception. The Soul enters the Now-World from the East.

Through the Guardians of the East comes special Atisokanak-related knowledge. The Elders also said that East is the source of a unique and powerful energy which is more volatile than the energy based in the other directions. It is the "place" of the Contraries who rely upon this energy to demonstrate the tenuous balance of positive and negative aspects inherent in human nature.

South always come next. From this direction comes Atisokanak-inspired creativity. The Elders also said that South is the source of Atisokanak-conferred benevolence, growth, and maturity.

The third in order is West, the direction of death for a Now-World body. When one's Soul leaves the body, it is said "to west" over Atisokanak water.

Continuing in a circle, the next direction is North. North is thought of as a place of healing and of preparation for renewal in East (if the Atisokanak Life-Form Masters conclude that reincarnation is necessary). This direction is also the home of "Bear Power," which is a healing power. The Elders said that the Northern Lights come out to dance at those times when "Bear Power" is most potent. Sweetgrass, a fragrant plant also associated with "Bear Power," comes from the Atisokanak Guardian of the North and is used to keep away negative energies.

The fifth direction is "below" or "within the Earth." It is especially close to the heart of Earth Mother, whom we all depend upon for life.

"Above" or "outward" is the sixth direction. It represents the above-worlds and includes the Sun which nurtures the Earth and all of Her creatures.

The seventh and last direction is "within the self." This direction is very important because it is the point of reference for the other directions. All directions converge within the self and project outward from this same point. If an individual is not centered in primal balance within the self, there can be no context for the other directions to exist. Without such a context, it is not possible for the individual to maintain 'balance'.

Each of the four cardinal points of the Seven Sacred Directions has a special Atisokanak World Guardian who emphasizes the female aspect of the universal oneness.

PIPE CEREMONY

The Elders pointed out that the *Pipe Ceremony* is symbolic of and perpetuates the love and respect that humans are to show Earth Mother. The pipe itself represents the interdependency of all created beings whose lives are inextricably linked to each other through Great Spirit. These beings are symbolically united in the making of the pipe and the performance of the ceremony. From the Rock-People comes the material for the bowl of the pipe. From the Plant-People come the smoking substance and the material for the stem of the pipe. The humans performing the ceremony are the representatives for the world of flesh.

In the ceremony, the first puff of smoke is offered to Great Spirit. The second puff is offered to Earth Mother and the four primary elements in Earth Mother. Following this, a puff of smoke is offered slowly and reverently to each of the four winds and each spirit of the Seven Sacred Directions.

The burning of Kinnikinnick or tobacco is symbolic of the ongoing cycles of creation and destruction, life and death, and the continual changes taking place in form and substance in the Now-World. The Pipe Ceremony, then, is a rite of communion with the Great Spirit through all elements of the ongoing process of creation. It is a ritual way of reaffirming the interconnection of the self with the universal-all, in turn providing a balanced perspective from which to apprehend the reality of both the Now-World and Atisokanak World.

NOTES

1. Johnston, *Ojibway Heritage*, 25.

2. Ibid.

3. Edward Benton-Banai, *The Mishomis Book: The Voice of the Ojibway*, (St. Paul: Indian Country Press, 1979), 17.

4. Johnston, *Ojibway Heritage*, 109-118. Basil includes an excellent story explaining the Four Hills of Life on these pages.

5. This version is based on a version which was recorded in the field notes of Fletcher and La Flesche, *Bureau of American Ethnology 27th Annual Report*, 1911, 115-116.

CHAPTER FIVE
THE STAR PEOPLE

The Elders sometimes talked about immense flying objects seen very high in the sky which resembled enormous birds and made a sound which sounded like, but was not, thunder. On those rare occasions when these objects were observed from a closer vantage point, it seemed as if they had eyes which flashed like lightning. The Western Great Lakes American Indian tradition has quite a few stories about these "great birds" whose home on Earth was thought to be far to the west.

The Elders said that long ago, according to *their* Elders, a party of hunters, upon entering a large forest clearing, saw an enormous shiny object that appeared to have fog rising from it. The hunters could see flashes like lightning coming from the center of the "fog." As much as they wanted to know what the object was, none of them dared approach it, fearful of what would happen if they did. The next day, however, some of the hunters returned to the clearing to try to determine what it was that they had seen. But again fear overcame them as soon as they saw the object, and once more they left without finding out what it was. When they went back the third day--the object was gone! Where it had been there was now a large scorched area.

What the hunters had seen, the Elders said, was something that they called a "Thunderbird" and is in actuality a relatively small flying vehicle of the Star People.

In the summer of 1988, while doing historical research in the Upper Peninsula of Michigan, I had the opportunity to investigate a unique circle of stones on the largest island of a group located between the Upper and Lower Peninsulas. This recently discovered circle, referred to by media sources in Michigan as "Michigan's Stonehenge," has a diameter of approximately 397 feet.

The extraordinary circle was discovered about four years ago by a woman who was a school teacher on the island. I spent some time investigating the circle with her, returning to the site several times before returning to Wisconsin. For the past two years a group of scholars representing several academic disciplines has been investigating this same site.

The structure of the stone circle is remarkable. Unusually symmetrical, there are four immense rocks located precisely at each cardinal point. The colossal center rock has an eight-inch hole bored into the top. Another large marker-rock denotes the location of the North Star at the time of the sunrise during the summer solstice. Certain other rock formations and/or locations appear to chart various constellations. Hieroglyphic-like markings and pictographs on several rocks seem to denote astronomical symbols and locations.

Test boring throughout the circumference of the circle area demonstrates that there is a large *charred* circular area that does not exceed the perimeter of the stone circle.

When I entered the circle area the first time, and each time thereafter, I found myself thinking that this circle is the same one described in 1856 by Henry R. Schoolcraft in the story, "The Star Family, or Celestial Sisters."[1] While Schoolcraft probably incorrectly attributed the source of this story to Shawnee legend, the same or similar story was told by many tribal groups. The Elders from whom I learned said the story was based on a true event which took place a very long time ago on a group of islands located northeast of Wisconsin in the Western Great Lakes.

The following story was told by my Elders and is quite similar to the one Schoolcraft recorded. Both make reference to a circle like the one on the island in Michigan:

> One day a young man who lived with his family in a remote area of the forest wandered into unfamiliar territory and found himself at the edge of an unusual clearing. In the middle of the clearing was a large charred area in the shape of a circle. Outside of the circular area was another circle which appeared to be made by footsteps following the same tracks over a long period of time. The young man knew his discovery was special because he could see no path in the clearing leading to or from the circle.
>
> He would return to this place periodically and conceal himself in the brush at the edge of the clearing while he watched and waited, hoping to discover how this strange circle came to be. One day while he was hiding he noticed what appeared to be a flash--like that of a twinkling star--in the blue of the afternoon sky. The flash soon became a small, descending shiny object. As it came closer, he heard the faint sound of music. It sounded as if the music were coming from the skies. Looking up once more he saw that the object was coming closer and he quickly realized it was larger than he originally thought it to be. Soon he understood that he was looking at some kind of sky-craft and that this was the source of the ethereal music which filled his ears. The craft landed in the charred center of the well-worn circle. The young man watched in amazement as twelve beautiful, human-like women descended from the craft, entered the area of the circle, and began to dance to the marvelously enchanting music. When the dancers realized there was someone watching them, they ran back into the craft which started slowly to rise and then suddenly disappeared into the sky. The outline of the charred circle had been freshly scorched by the departing craft.
>
> The young man returned home and told his parents what he had witnessed. The story awakened in his mother a memory of something her grandmother had told

her when she was a girl. She turned to her son and explained that he had seen some of the Star People who have very special abilities. When the young man told his mother that he felt as if he could easily fall in love with one of these wondrous females, she felt a twinge of alarm seize her body. She cautioned him that a Star Woman would not be content to stay on Earth. In addition she said that the Star People were not affected by the same time and spatial constraints that humans were; consequently, she would not age at the same rate that he did.

She explained that he would grow old and quite immobile, while the Star Woman remained relatively young. Finally she asked him if he felt that such differences could result in lasting happiness. The young man listened and thought for a long time about what his mother told him, but still it could not keep him from feeling drawn back to the special clearing he had found.

Over time the young man observed the phenomenon of the first day regularly. Eventually he won the friendship and finally the love of one of the beautiful female beings who danced to the exquisite music in the clearing. He fathered a child by her and later left with her and the child, bound for her father's home on a planet in the system of a distant star. The Elders said that no one is sure what happened to him; however, some say he, and later his descendants, would periodically return to Earth to observe what is happening here.

The stone circle in Michigan also appears to be related to another story which the Elders told and which Schoolcraft also recorded under the title, "The Son of the Evening Star." The story is about a family in a tribal group living in the Western Great Lakes area:

Living in a village near the lake there was a family with ten beautiful daughters. The youngest daughter was the most beautiful of all. But she, unlike her sisters, was not interested in the many men who came courting. She instead loved the beautiful, special, and secluded natural places near her home. Even after all of her sisters had married, the youngest and most beautiful daughter continued to ignore her suitors, preferring to spend her time in the special places she loved so much.

Her family often criticized her and warned her that some day she would end up being alone with no chance left of ever getting married.

Then one day an old man, who was scarcely able to walk and obviously very poor, came to call on her. Soon he was visiting every day and it became evident that the youngest daughter very much enjoyed spending her time with the strange and enfeebled old man. Her family simply could not understand her bizarre behavior and, needless to say, they were completely shocked when the daughter announced that she had agreed to marry him!

She insisted that this was her choice and soon after, she married him despite the family's efforts to dissuade her. Many in the village laughed at her and taunted her for having made such a terrible choice of a husband, especially when she had been seriously courted by so many handsome, young, and promisingly prosperous men.

Nevertheless, the daughter seemed to be very happy, telling those who laughed at her and taunted her, ''It was my choice. You will see in the end who has acted the wisest.''

Shortly thereafter the entire family, including the bizarre couple, was invited to a special feast some distance from their village.

As they all walked along the trail toward the place of the feast, many family members could not help pitying the youngest of the sisters for having made such a terrible choice for her life's mate. This was especially apparent to the family when the old husband kept stopping and looking into the skies while muttering something which was, to the rest of the family, unintelligible. When they looked into the sky to see what he kept looking at, all they could see was a faint flicker that they thought was the Evening Star.

Finally the group came to the place of the feast. They saw that the feasting lodge appeared to be made of some kind of strange metal and was unlike any that they had ever seen before; yet, they entered this strange lodge so as not to offend their host, who they really didn't know, but about whom they had heard wondrous things.

As soon as they entered the strange lodge, it began to shudder and then seemed to lift away from the ground. The family soon realized that the lodge had indeed lifted off the ground and--not only that--it was moving up and away from the Earth!

The youngest daughter's husband then uttered a joyous sound. When the entire family turned to look at him, they were astonished to see that his appearance had been almost completely transformed. Rather than the old, crippled man he had been, he now appeared to be one of the most handsome young men any of them had ever seen. He explained to them that he was not from Earth and that while on Earth his physiological processes had been affected by the planet's composition and gravity which in turn had drastically altered his original appearance.

Finally they came to another world, somewhat like the Earth, but far from the Earth in another star system. There they learned from the husband's people that some other beings who tended to serve evil had left him stranded on Earth causing his predicament. They also were told that, obviously, their kind needed some additional guidance since by failing to accept their in-law in the form of the old man, they had demonstrated that they were not sensitive enough to perceive the lack of balance in their own lives. His people explained that a group of beings from their world would be sent with the family back to the Earth to try to provide the necessary guidance needed there.

When it came time to meet those who had been chosen to accompany them back to the Earth, the family saw that their companions were very small. The humans were told that these beings were called the "Paueeseegug" or "Little People."

They were then directed to follow the Paueeseegug into a craft similar to the one that brought them to the faraway planet. Shortly thereafter the craft began to rise and the family knew they were on their way back to the Earth.

When the craft was over the upper Lake Michigan area, it began to descend slowly. Finally it hovered over a group of islands located between the present-day Upper and Lower Peninsulas of Michigan.

The craft came to a stop on the highest of the group of islands. It is said that to this day the Paueeseegug still live in that island group and that sometimes they may even be seen dancing and singing on the moonlit beaches--if they are not disturbed by the humans who are observing them.

In the Western Great Lakes American Indian oral tradition there are many other references in the ancient stories and legends to the Star People who visited and interacted with people on Earth.

The Elders told of other beings who looked somewhat like the American Indians except that they had much fairer skin and were definitely *not* human. The Elders said that these "people" had the responsibility of guarding the heavens in the area of Earth. They were called the "Heaven People" and dressed in scarlet tunics with a hood.

The Elders said that one day an old man of about ninety told the people of his village that he was going to "die" the next day. When asked how he knew, he said that one of the "Heaven People" had told him so in a dream. He told the villagers that they were not to bury his body. Instead, they were to take it to a certain island in the big lake. There they were to lay his body on the beach and wait. He said that the Heaven People would come and take it away.

The next morning, just as he had predicted, the elder was dead. The villagers did as he had requested, although some of them thought it all seemed quite bizarre. As they waited on the beach of the small island that the old man had specified before his death, they suddenly heard what sounded like thunder. Yet there were no clouds in the sky. Then, the sound of a great wind roared above them.

Soon a strange, shiny craft appeared directly over the beach. From the craft four human-like beings appeared, each dressed in scarlet clothing with hoods drawn over their heads. They approached the elder's body where it lay on the beach. One of them took the hand of the dead body and the old man suddenly rose, looked at the villagers, then smiled and ascended into the craft with the four Heaven People. The craft then slowly rose and, with a loud thunderous sound, vanished from sight.

The Star People also figure prominently in the stories about Nokomis who was the grandmother of the first human. In these stories and legends it is clear that Nokomis is *not* from Earth! She and her daughter, the mother of the first human, are said to be from the East, beyond the Earth, from a place referred to as the "Morning Star."

The Morning Star nowadays is identified as the planet Venus; however, in the ancient time referred to here, the Morning Star was identified as the planet between Mars and Jupiter, where an asteroid belt is now. According to several ancient traditions, the belt was created as a result of a massive collision between that ancient Morning Star planet, called "Tiamat," and an "intruder" astronomical body. This collision took place during a time referred to in many legends as the time of "The War in the Heavens."

The Elders told of how some of the beings from the Morning Star, who begot the first humans, were offended when later the humans did not remember to honor them appropriately. In their anger they emerged from their base in the west with a noise which reverberated across the heavens. Obscured by clouds, they crossed directly over the homes and the villages of the forgetful humans and in their fury they shot what looked like bolts of lightning at the earth below. Finally, the humans learned to honor their ancestors from another planet appropriately. Although this happened in the distant past, humans continued symbolically to honor the memory of the people from the Morning Star by reverently offering Kinnikinnick each time that a thunder storm rumbled through. The storms sounded like the crafts of those ancient ancestral beings.

The Elders stated that these legends and stories are all that remain of a recollection of the time when the Star People in their skycrafts regularly came out of the western skies, especially during "The War in the Heavens," and directed light beam weaponry (which resembled lightning) at colonies of their enemies. The great rumbling heard on earth was the sound of their sky-craft as it approached and then passed overhead.

Another legend tells of a time when a serious quarrel arose between the beings called "Underwater Panthers" and some other beings called "Thunderbirds." The Underwater Panthers had a "den" in the depths of what is now called Devils Lake, in Sauk County, Wisconsin. The legend states that the Thunderbirds hurled "thunderbolt arrows" into the waters and onto the bluffs surrounding the lake. The Underwater Panthers "threw" great "rocks" upward from beneath the waters of the lake in an attempt to hit the Thunderbirds. A terrible battle continued for days. The tumbled down and cracked rocky surface of the bluffs surrounding the lake are evidence of the great struggle. Finally the Thunderbirds were victorious and soon afterward they flew away to their "nests" in the northwest.

No American Indians would approach that lake for a long time. It is said that the Underwater Panthers were not all killed during the war and that some still live in Devils Lake to this day.

Later, American Indian peoples living in the area not too far from the lake, as well as travelers from afar, had a custom of making Kinnikinnick offerings to the "spirits" of the lake. They would deposit their offerings on boulders along the shore or place them on the surface of the water.

The Elders said that stories like the preceding one are memory-remnants of actual accounts of the fiery sky battles between two very different forms of Star People.

It was believed, according to the Elders, that at one time in the ancient past the Thunderbirds had a huge "nest" in the then-mountainous area around Lake Nipigon, northeast of Duluth, Minnesota, in Ontario. They said that, according to legend, large blankets of clouds always covered the "nest." The native people in the region considered this "nest" area to be a sacred place and did not go there. Consequently, they did not really know what the Star People were doing in that area.

According to the Elders, some years before the coming of the Europeans, the blanket of clouds began to lift and move away. At that time the Thunderbirds destroyed every trace of the place, pretty nearly leveling a large portion of the mountains in the process.

The Elders also said that, in ancient times, there were humanoid-appearing "Water Beings" in the Great Lakes area. They also were related to the Star People. These Water Beings sometimes approached humans and instructed them by communicating through telepathy. Their crafts were very different from the water crafts of the humans. Long ago, human ancestors erected offering rocks for the Water Beings at various areas along the shorelines. One such offering rock lies at the northwest point of Medicine Island. The Elders said that, since the coming of the Europeans, the Water Beings almost never appear; however, it is believed that these beings are still here. Once in a while if someone is caught in a storm and reverently makes an offering, the Water Beings may help calm the waters.

The Elders said that the original humanoid was lowered to Earth from a starship. They said that the initial Earth home for "Original Man" was a large land mass which was located east of Central and South America in the mid-Atlantic--a land mass that obviously is not there now. They explained that the area was destroyed when an almost world-wide flood completely covered the land mass. It is still under the waters of the mid-Atlantic. (This area, incidentally, is part of the area destroyed due to the misuse of power referred to in the second story of chapter three.) The Elders said that the word "Anishinabeg" originally referred to "the People who came from beyond where the sun rises."

Original Man, humanoid but not human, is a hybrid who embodies some of the most negative qualities of his human ancestors and some of the most positive qualities of his Star People relatives. Often considered a nefarious character, he is in actuality neither all bad nor all good, but simply a reflection of both. Because of this, he is what some scholars refer to as the culture hero or trickster.

Original Man spent quite a good deal of time visiting and learning from Nokomis while she was still living on the Earth. Later Nokomis, like her daughter, left the Earth to live elsewhere in the universe.

Whenever the moon is visible in the skies at night, and especially when it is full, humans are to remember Nokomis and her special role as "grandmother" to all human beings.

STAR PEOPLE: FROM THE PERSPECTIVE OF MODERN SCIENCE

In the branch of metaphysics called ontology, the nature of 'being' in the universe is approached by asking questions about the kinds of beings that may exist, or the nature of these beings, or whether any possible relationship could exist between such beings.

American Indians of the Great Lakes region answered these ontological questions in their ancient legends and stories. It is clear that, like native peoples throughout the world, they believed in the existence of other-world beings. Their stories also suggest that communication and interaction between humans and those other-world beings occurred. There must be some reason beyond mere coincidence that explains why this commonly held metaphysical belief occurs in so many ancient human societies.

Contemporary theoretical scientists, especially those involved in planning the exploration of space, ask the same ontological questions as the ancient tribal peoples, but from another perspective.

In July of 1989, the National Aeronautics and Space Administration (NASA) awarded a three-year grant to the School of Architecture and Urban Planning at the University of Wisconsin-Milwaukee to support research related to designing work-space and living quarters for planned colonies on the Moon and Mars. Other United States universities are also involved in research concerning the exploration of space and proposed expeditions to Mars. If we possess the technology on Earth to make other planets suitable for habitation by humans, then is it not possible that other beings may have done the same on Earth? Could it be that the existence of the Star People is theoretically possible from the perspective of modern scientific knowledge? Why else would the space probe Voyager, which will eventually leave our solar system, contain pictures of what we look like, a map of our solar system and Earth's position in it, and technological information in formulae, if those people working on the project did not believe that the existence of other life-forms were possible?

In 1981, Professor Francis Crick, who won the Nobel Prize for Physiology in 1962 for his work on DNA, wrote *Life Itself: It's Origin and Nature* [2] in which he describes our vast universe containing at least ten billion galaxies, each of which has stars that resemble our star, the Sun. In our galaxy alone, the Milky Way galaxy, there are somewhere near one hundred billion stars.

Based on these observations, Crick asserts that it is logical to assume that many stars in the universe have planets orbiting them and that a significant number of those planets have the conditions necessary for sustaining some form of life.

Crick postulates that "thinking life" must have evolved on a percentage of these planets. He states that it is logical to assume that on some of these planets scientific and technological developments may also have taken place.

It also follows that some of these developments may be far beyond anything humans have accomplished to date, and may include the ability to travel to neighboring planets, or to nearby star systems, and possibly into other galaxies.

Crick speculates that peoples from one or more of these worlds may have known that their own civilizations were, for whatever reason, doomed. Perhaps they had found that a neighboring star was set on a collision course with theirs or that their own sun was going to become a red giant that would eventually engulf their planet.

He states that it is possible, perhaps even likely, that inter-space flight did occur wherein highly advanced beings traveled and colonized other planets in other star systems, and that upon arriving at these new planets, they may have had to carry out extensive genetic engineering in order to exist given the environmental peculiarities of the planet.

According to Crick, we cannot rule out the possibility that large spacecraft (mother-craft) maintained, and perhaps still maintain, orbits in places where they would be difficult to detect--near Neptune, for instance, or in the asteroid belt between Jupiter and Mars. These beings have probably made, perhaps still make, forays in smaller crafts to planets in our solar system, including Earth, to obtain needed minerals and other raw materials, as well as to observe.

Crick concludes that it may be "dangerous" for us to assume that we are "alone" in the universe and that we should be cautious about our actions on this planet lest we run the risk of being perceived as about to "contaminate the galaxy"[3] through environmental and technological abuse.

It is interesting to note that, just as the Elders pointed out, Professor Crick also stresses the need for balance in our daily actions by acknowledging the possible existence of other beings who share our universe. Events on our planet have repercussions in the universe which twentieth century scientists are only beginning to understand. If there were nothing else than this to learn from the stories told here, they would still be invaluable. Let us hope that the Star People will not have to hold us accountable when one day our planet faces destruction because we refused to believe people like Crick and because we ignored the ancient stories of the Elders.

NOTES

1. Henry R. Schoolcraft, *The Myth of Hiawatha and Other Oral Legends...of the North American Indians*, (Philadelphia: J. B. Lippincott & Co., 1856), 71-76, 116-120, 299-301.

2. Francis Crick, *Life Itself: It's Origin and Nature*, (New York: Simon and Schuster, 1981).

3. Ibid., 160, 167-170.

CHAPTER SIX
THE INHERENT PRIMACY OF FEMALE BEINGS

The Elders taught that, by the design of Great Spirit, female beings have primacy over males. Their preeminence is due to the female's integral and intimate participation in the continually manifesting sacred cycle of creation, destruction, and re-creation. As a result, all female beings symbolize and embody a portion of Great Spirit's life-giving force.

Likewise, female beings are said to be automatic conduits for "power" from the Atisokanak World.

Edward Benton-Banai, a member of the Lac Courte Oreilles Band of the Lake Superior Ojibway, reinforces many of the oral traditions regarding the primacy of the female in *The Mishomis Book: The Voice of the Ojibway*. He, like the Elders who taught me, makes it clear that according to oral tradition, female beings *preceded* male beings on the Earth at the time of creation. In addition, Great Spirit utilizes females to cast the "Light of Knowledge" on males. Females are the ones who come first and "light the way" for males, who, because they are not created with an automatic connection to the Atisokanak World, and therefore not completely developed, need the "light" that females provide to make them "whole."[1]

Basil Johnston also emphasizes the "veneration for the primacy of womanhood":

> [W]henever the moon shown in the heavens...the primacy of womanhood [is] remembered....[F]or it was through woman that the cycle--creation, destruction, re-creation--was completed. Women had a special place in the order of existence and were exempt from the vision quest.[2]

Some non-American Indian scholars contend that tribal peoples ascribed relatively inferior roles to females and that women could be religious leaders only in very exceptional situations, and even then, they had to be subordinate to male religious leaders. These same scholars also misguidedly write that a young woman's Vision Quest experiences were, if they occurred, far less powerful than those of young men. The reader should note that the scholars who came to these conclusions during fieldwork often received their information from American Indians who were either

Christians themselves or were heavily influenced by the Christian tradition. Had the scholars established a meaningful rapport with non-Christian tribal Elders who still practiced the old religions, and asked them to explain the role of women in American Indian traditions, they may have learned some of things which I did.

The Elders taught that in the oral tradition of the Western Great Lakes Indians, women played very prominent roles in religious life; that is, prior to the intrusion of the Christian missionaries.

Most Western scholars come from male-dominated societies with patriarchal world views. Even female scholars at times have difficulty transcending this societal bias. Once again, if one cannot suspend one's own cultural prepossessions when viewing another culture, it is easy to miss things which seem inconsequential to the observer yet are fundamental for the participant. Early scholars and others were so culturally biased that they did not, perhaps could not, *see* what was in front of them. They did not see the importance of the female in religious functioning, either because they did not want to see it, or more likely, because they had not been trained to see it.

The Elders told a story of how long ago a band of tribal people were moving about during the fall hunt. One small girl was constantly crying because she was so lonely and did not have any sisters or brothers to play with. Her mother, in an attempt to hush her, kept threatening to give her to the owls.

Now, it just so happened that some owls heard the mother and they asked their leader, Grandmother Owl, "Why don't we take the child? She has been offered to us many times." Finally one day, after a particularly long period of fretting and crying, the mother grabbed the little girl and carried her to the edge of the clearing and placed her down saying, "Owls, come and get her. She's yours."

The others in the camp heard the little girl cry for a time and then there was complete silence. Finally, the mother went out to see if her daughter had fallen asleep crying. The little girl was gone! The mother went from lodge to lodge looking for her daughter, but she could find no trace of her.

The little girl was with the Owl-People, keeping comfortable and warm. They made sure that she was fed well and tried to keep her as happy as owls are able. Periodically the girl would mention that she might want to go back, but for now she was content where she was.

One day Grandmother Owl told the girl that the owls were going to bring her back to the human community. Grandmother Owl said that she would also be given a special gift before she went back. It was a special hunting "medicine" which, if used properly, would charm deer and other game and assure a successful hunt when truly needed. The Grandmother Owl then told the girl that from now on the only way for humans to obtain this particular kind of hunting medicine was from a young girl who would play a special role in its preparation and delivery.

The owls took the young girl, who had been gone almost an entire year, back to the humans. Needless to say, her mother and the other villagers were shocked to find her sitting in the village area. They were especially surprised to see that she had been cared for so well. The young girl told the villagers that she had been given a special gift from Grandmother Owl. She said that it was to be a reminder to humans that they must be careful of what they ask for because the other life-forms might very well grant them their wish. Furthermore, the only way that humans could obtain this gift in the future was with the help of a young girl. She said that this also was to be a continual reminder to the human community that all female beings have primacy in the universe of Great Spirit.

Some of the Elders told the story of Leelinau, the beautiful young daughter of one of the leaders of a tribal group from the islands between the Lower and Upper Peninsulas of Michigan. According to the story, she paid little heed to the attentions of all the males who attempted to court her. She instead preferred to wander along the beach alone, often stopping in lovely areas to relax and enjoy the solitude. As more and more suitors pressured her, she grew more and more alienated from the everyday world around her. Leelinau's mother often warned her about the possible dangers of spending so much time alone in those places, reminding her that those were the places of the Little People (the Paueeseegug). The mother said that one of these days the Little People would take her away. She also began pressuring Leelinau to accept the attentions of one of the fine men who came calling for her.

Finally, the young woman agreed to marry the handsome son of a renowned tribal leader from a neighboring group. On the day of the wedding, she dressed in her bridal finery then asked her mother to allow her one final opportunity to go alone briefly to one of her favorite places on the beach. Her mother reluctantly agreed and she was off.

Back at the village everyone waited for her. They waited in vain. Some fishermen later said that they had seen a beautiful young woman walking along the beach with some of the Little People and that she then walked off into the forest with them. Leelinau was never seen again--except that fishermen sometimes report sighting her dancing on the beach with the Little People. Even to this day, boaters sometimes report seeing this same sight on moonlit nights. Sometimes vacationers also report finding footprints in the sand dunes along the Lake Michigan shoreline. One set of prints is obviously that of a young human. The others appear to be unrealistically tiny!

Finally, the Elders told a story about two young men who went out hunting. They were not having any luck, so one of the young men suggested climbing to the top of a nearby hill in order to see if they could spot some deer. They both climbed to the top of the hill and looked in all directions, but they didn't see any game.

They did see, however, what appeared to be a small figure some distance from where they were. The two hunters sat and watched as the figure moved toward the hill.

As the figure came closer, they realized that it was actually a beautiful woman. She appeared to be almost gliding over the surface of the forest. In her hands she carried a small bundle.

One of the young men, looking suggestively at her as she approached, told his companion that he desired the woman. The other young man told him that he sensed that she was somehow different; that she might be related to the Atisokanak World in some way, or that perhaps she was a Star Woman. He told his companion that he felt it was a grave mistake to think of the approaching woman as a sexual object. The first young man scoffed at him and said, "I'll show you. Wait 'til she is within speaking range!"

When the beautiful young woman was within speaking range, she looked at both of them, then back at the young man who wanted her. She smiled a strange kind of alluring smile and said to him, "Come, you shall have what you desire!"

The first young man approached her, and as he did, a fog-like cloud enveloped the couple. His companion wondered what was happening, but he dared not approach.

Finally the cloud dissipated. The waiting young man was shocked to see the strange young woman standing alone. At her feet lay a human skeleton covered with crawling worms.

She pointed to the skeleton and said to the second hunter, "He had what he desired. Do not be afraid; go back to your village and tell your people that I will be there shortly to give to them a special gift from my world."

(At this point in the story, the Elders would remind us that one must be careful when encountering "people" who may not be from the Now-World Earth. Trying to take advantage of such "persons" may be dangerous--at the very least.)

The surviving young man hurried back to his village and told the people what he had seen and what had just happened. Then, the villagers heard a shout and one of the men working at the edge of the village pointed toward the forest. There, emerging into the clearing, was the beautiful woman. As she approached the village, her feet seemed to glide over the surface of the Earth as though she were floating.

She stood before the villagers, radiantly beautiful, her voice like the song of a stream splashing over the rocks in springtime. Her eyes seemed to look into their very Souls.

She took a stick and drew seven circles on the earth and said, "I have drawn seven circles. They represent the Seven Sacred Directions of the Atisokanak. Do not forget them!" She unwrapped the small bundle and presented a beautifully carved ceremonial pipe to them. Then she said, "Use this pipe to honor the Spirit-World. Use it to worship Gitchi Manitou."

She then told them that she was going to have to leave and warned the villagers that a time would come when, invaded, disturbed, and oppressed by outsiders from another part of the Earth, their descendants would almost lose their sacred traditions; but that, if there were those who sincerely tried to keep the old ways alive, the traditions would not disappear. She continued by saying that after a long time, after the bearded star crossed the heavens many times, after Spirit Lake disappeared, the great mountains spewed forth, and the Turtle (who supports the Earth) shook herself, she would return with her people who had been among the ancestors of the villagers long before she came. With those words she walked toward the forest edge and vanished from sight. Some ran after her, trying to catch her, but they could find no sign of her trail. It was almost as if she had never been there at all. But she had been there--that they knew--for they still had the ceremonial pipe which she had left with them.

The Elders who told and retold this story said that the woman was not an Atisokanak Person, but rather that she was a Star Woman from a people who possessed a great deal of very powerful Atisokanak abilities. She foresaw the future which, although grim, offers hope to those who remember to honor Gitchi Manitou.

The time when the Turtle shakes herself may be fast approaching. The sacred traditions survive only through the strength of those with the vision to see how out-of-balance the human world is becoming. The daughters must once again come forward and save their Mother. They must remember the meaning of the sacred pipe.

The Elders said that certain females, as well as a very few special males, have been given a unique Atisokanak gift which enables them to sense the feelings of other species--including the feelings of the Plant-People. They said that these special individuals can hear what they called the *si-si-gwad*, the crying of the forest when an imbalance is created by an act of a human.

All over the planet the forests are crying; and Earth Mother cries along. The stresses that many sensitive people feel today may be in part caused by this ability to hear these sounds which have gone unrecognized for so long and are often only perceived at the level of the subconscious. How does one begin the process of reincorporating these gifts back into the level of consciousness? The Elders said in this regard that whenever there are those who ask questions, *there will always be those who remember.*

Recently, researchers with the United States Forest Service fastened special sensors to the bark of drought-stricken trees and reported clearly picking up what appeared to be distress emanations.

It appears that, once again, the Elders knew something that has taken the present-day technological society a long time to discover.

It is time to ask questions. It is time to remember.

NOTES

1. Benton-Banai, *The Mishomis Book: The Voice of the Ojibway*, 2, 37.
2. Johnston, *Ojibway Heritage*, 17, 24, 26.

GLOSSARY

The cultures of the American Indian peoples living in the Western Great Lakes region are both rich and varied. The languages of each tribe, while related, are diverse and reflective of those values of individual importance to a particular tribe. The words defined here may have other meanings which are just as valid. In cases where a word has more than one meaning, or may be expressed by a different word altogether, the decision, while difficult to make, was based upon choosing a definition which would be in keeping with the teachings of my Elders.

Animikeeg: meaning "Thunderers" in the Algonquian languages, they are among the Atisokanak People who possess the greatest "power" potential and are at the top of the Atisokanak hierarchy. They may manifest in the Now-Worlds in the form of eagles, clouds, lightning, and the sound of thunder and other loud noises.

Anishinabeg: meaning "the People who came from beyond where the sun rises," the name refers to the original human inhabitants of the earth.

apparitions: manifestations caused by the continued presence of the ghost-portion of an individual's Spirit after the death of the physical body.

Ashkibewig: the Atisokanak Persons who help Great Spirit with specific aspects of the creation process. Their name translates as "Helpers."

Atisokanak Guardians: the Atisokanak Persons who appear to an individual at the time of the Vision Quest to offer continuing support and guidance during the individual's life on Earth.

Atisokanak Persons/People: spirit-beings inhabiting the Atisokanak World who interact with human beings and provide the means to channel "power" from the Atisokanak World into a Now-World. Their dispositions may be either benevolent or malevolent in nature. There are three main types of Atisokanak Persons: Discarnate Entities, Souls Previously Incarnate in a Now-World, and Life-Form Masters. All Atisokanak Persons are more "powerful" than Now-World People.

Atisokanak World: a multidimensional energy world which is the source of all "power" flowing into Now-Worlds such as Earth. It is the home of the Atisokanak Persons and is the site of the final resting place for departed Souls.

balance: a state of being in which the positive aspects of the universe equal the negative aspects. This principal governs all actions in the universe from the microcosmic to the macrocosmic level.

Bear: greatly respected in Western Great Lakes American Indian metaphysics not simply because of its apparent size and strength, but because of the principal role it played in establishing the Tree of Life as a channel of communication between the two worlds above and below the earth. Often addressed as "Grandmother" or "Grandfather," it is human-like in its ability to stand upright. The bear is also associated with the potent healing power which originates in the North.

Bear-Walking: the shamanistic ability to metamorphose into the form of a bear.

center/centering: the process of achieving a state of harmonious balance which reflects the original balanced state of the Now-World upon its creation.

circle: a sacred and universal symbol representing both the Creator and the created in one. The circular shape and arc of both the Moon and the Sun (as seen from Earth) serve as constant reminders of the cyclic nature of the universe.

clairvoyance: the ability to obtain information about a particular person by focusing on an object or location associated with the individual. The perception of this information is sensory.

conduit: a Now-World person through whom "power" from the Atisokanak World travels and manifests in a Now-World.

cosmology: a branch of metaphysics dealing with the way people perceive the nature and order of the universe.

culture hero: an individual of human and Star Person ancestry who paradoxically exhibits the worst of all human qualities and the best attributes of the Star People.

Discarnate Entities: Atisokanak Persons who have never entered a Now-World body. There are two subtypes of Discarnate Entities: The first includes Atisokanak Persons who will never take on substantive form. The second subtype includes Souls that have not yet but will eventually enter a Now-World body.

doorkeepers: Atisokanak guardians of the hierophanies who may either assist or prevent passage into the Atisokanak World. They are often female.

double vision: the ability to recognize aspects of the Atisokanak World in the Now-World through the understanding of the way in which each of these distinct worlds relates to the other.

Dreams: a combination social situation and educational experience in which the ghost-portion of the Spirit travels to the Atisokanak World in order to communicate with the Atisokanak People while the body is in a state of sleep.

Eagle: greatly respected Now-World Person who serves as a messenger between human beings and the Thunderers. Eagle's compassion for human beings saved the early human communities from destruction by Great Spirit.

effigies: handmade images of an individual used in the practice of sympathetic magic.

ESP: see **extrasensory perception**

ethnocentric: characteristic of the belief that one's own ethnic or racial group is superior to others.

Eurocentric: oriented toward European values and beliefs to the exclusion of any other possible interpretation of human belief systems.

extrasensory perception: a receptive and informational psychic phenomenon.

Four Hills of Life: a metaphorical way of describing the stages of life; childhood, adolescence, adulthood, and old age as though each were a hill to climb.

four primary elements: fire, air, water, and earth: the first things Great Spirit created in the universe. Each element has a unique Soul-Spirit subject to the amoral and dual nature of the universe and may manifest in either a positive or negative manner.

Four Winds: The Now-World Persons; Wabanodin (East Wind), Shawanodin (South Wind), Ningaabinodin (West Wind), and Keewaedinodin (North Wind), who are responsible for the changes in seasons and weather.

Four Winds Cross: symbol of universal balance as represented by the plus sign (+).

gatekeeper: see **doorkeeper**

Geezis: the name for the Sun in the Algonquian languages.

Ghost: the portion of the Spirit which may travel outside of the body during Dream and Vision experiences.

Gitchi Manitou: the "Great Spirit": the Supreme Being and Creator of the universe who is both male and female and is the source of the positive and negative energies that must continually be maintained in a 'balanced' state. Gitchi Manitou brought forth the universe through the process of dreaming.

Grandfather Rock: the respectful way to address a Rock-Person. The symbol of the unchanging Atisokanak World in a Now-World of constant change.

Great Spirit: see **Gitchi Manitou**

hauntings: a type of psychic phenomenon that occurs when individuals pick up recorded information about material beings or objects which is stored in the electromagnetic field surrounding all matter.

Heaven People: red-robed Star People who were long ago responsible for guarding the heavens in the area of the Earth.

hierophany: Atisokanak passageways located in wondrous natural places that serve to connect the Atisokanak World with the Now-Worlds.

karma: a word from the Sanskrit language meaning *fate* or *work*. It is used in the context of this book to describe Western Great Lakes American Indian metaphysical belief in the elastic-like ability of the universe to spring back into harmonious balance whenever the critical balance is disturbed.

Kinnikinnick: a mixture made from herbs which Great Spirit gave to the humans to use as an offering for the manitos.

Life-Form Master: an Atisokanak Person who is a spirit archetype serving as the nurturing caretaker and overseer of a particular species.

Little People: see **Paueeseegug**

Love Sorcery: the use of various plant and mineral substances to make one individual irresistibly attractive to another.

Mahng: the Anishinabeg word for both "brave" and "loon." In some Western Great Lakes oral traditions, Mahng is the embodiment of the laughter of Great

Spirit and the Spirit Helpers at the time of creation.

Manito: an Atisokanak Person who is interactively involved with Now-World beings and may serve as a Guardian Spirit. Manitos can exhibit either positive or negative behavior in their encounters with Now-World People. Like all other beings, they are subject to the will of Great Spirit.

Matchi Manitou: the name for a supreme evil spirit similar to the European notion of the Devil. The concept of Matchi Manitou appears have developed as a result of Christian influence upon American Indian tradition.

Mawandji: a concept which translates as "Remembering into the Future," and implies the cyclic nature of time as it is understood in Western Great Lakes American Indian metaphysics.

metamorphosis: conscious or unconscious change in outward appearance. A Now-World Person cannot accomplish metamorphosis without the aid of an Atisokanak Person.

metaphysics: a subdiscipline of philosophy concerned with the fundamental nature of reality and 'being'.

Misshipeshu: a powerful malevolent manito who sometimes appears in the form of a great horned cat.

monotheistic/monotheism: the belief that and characteristic of the belief that there is but one God.

Morning Star: in ancient times the planet Tiamat, the home of Nokomis, located between Jupiter and Mars. It was destroyed after colliding with another heavenly body during the time of "The War in the Heavens." The Morning Star nowadays is identified as the planet Venus.

Nokomis: the Star Person who was the grandmother of the first human, and also of "Original Man."

Now-World: a world where the pure energy of the Atisokanak World is mixed with matter. Earth is one of many Now-Worlds.

Now-World Persons/People: the inhabitants of a Now-World, including Plant-People, Animal-People, Cloud-People, Rock-People, the Star People, and human beings.

ontology: a branch of metaphysics dealing with questions relating to the types, natures, and relationships of beings in the universe.

Original Man: the grandson of Nokomis, humanoid but not human, whose positive attributes, inherited from his Star Person ancestors, are equally matched by the negative qualities inherited from his human relatives.

out-of-body-experience: the traveling of the ghost-portion of the Spirit outside of the body during Dreams and Visions.

Paueeseegug: smaller than human-size Star People who are said to inhabit special and secluded natural places on Earth.

Pipe Ceremony: a rite of communion with Great Spirit symbolically representing the ongoing cycles of life through the smoking of tobacco. The ceremony also is symbolic of and perpetuates the love and respect humans are to show Mother Earth and all of her Now-World children.

poltergeist: spontaneous psychokinetic outbursts caused by emotionally or psychologically disturbed individuals.

polytheistic/polytheism: the belief in or characteristic of the belief in more than one god.

possession: the use of a Now-World Person's body by an Atisokanak Person or Persons in order to facilitate Atisokanak interaction with other Now-World Persons--most often human beings.

power: the amoral, amorphous, and equally positive and negative energy force which pervades the universe. Power originates in Great Spirit and emanates only from the Atisokanak World.

precognition: the ability to perceive information which has not yet taken place in a linear segment of time.

principle of equal entitlement: a basic element of Western Great Lakes American Indian metaphysics which precludes the private ownership of land and assigns each individual the role of trustee over a small portion of the earth which will in turn be passed on to someone in the next generation. This principle assures that the Earth will always be cared for in a loving and balanced manner.

psychic phenomena: events perceived when the brain gains access to information outside of our limited perception of reality.

psychokinesis: an expressive, as opposed to receptive, psychic phenomenon involving the ability to move objects with the mind.

PSI: see **psychic phenomena**

quantum physics: a science based upon the idea that there is a basic oneness to the universe which can be subdivided into finite quanta. The oneness is thought of in terms of radiant energy.

reincarnation: the return of the Soul to a Now-World body in order to bring into balance business left unfinished or not corrected in a previous lifetime.

relativity theory: the theory based on the assumption that the speed of light in a vacuum is constant and independent of the source or observer, and that energy is equal to mass, and the change in mass, dimension, and time with increased velocity. The model universe, then, is four-dimensional continuum of space-time.

retrocognition: the ability to mentally gain access to information appearing to have taken place in the past.

Seven Sacred Directions: East, South, West, North, Above, Below, and Within. Each direction is associated with special "power" and knowledge which an individual may develop by orienting the self in that particular direction. The most important direction for each individual is "within the self" because it provides the individual with a reference point for each of the other directions.

shaman: a human being (male or female) who serves as a specialized technician in a conduit relationship with an Atisokanak Person. The shaman may use this powerful relationship in either a positive or negative manner.

si-si-gwad: the crying of the forest when an imbalance is created by human actions.

Soul: the life-sustaining portion of the Spirit. It is indestructible and immortal and carries with it an indelible record of all its memories and activities.

Spirit: the whole animating force within a body. It is composed of two aspects: the life-sustaining Soul, and the Ghost which may travel outside of the body.

Star People: Now-World People from distant planets and star systems who helped in the creation of the first human beings on Earth. In Western Great Lakes oral tradition, they have continuously interacted with human beings and have been a respected source of instruction and knowledge.

telekinesis: a type of psychokinesis (the ability to move things with the mind) whereby the object can actually be seen moving from one location to another.

telepathy: the awareness of information and/or emotions within another individual.

teleportation: a type of psychokinesis whereby an object moves from one location to another without actually being seen traveling the distance.

Thunder Stones: round, black stones related to the Thunderers' lightning-like bolts of energy. Thunder Stones are treated with special care and fresh offerings of Kinnikinnick must be placed with the stone four times a year.

Thunderbirds: small flying vehicles of the Star People. Also a generic name for the Star People living to the west of the Great Lakes area during "The War in the Heavens."

Thunderers: see **Animikeeg**

Tiamat: see **Morning Star**

Tibi-geezis: meaning "Night Sun," or " Moon," in the Algonquian languages.

tobacco: see **Kinnikinnick**

Totemic Animals: manitos, who, according to oral tradition, united with humans to form the first totemic clans: bear, rabbit, deer, etc.

Tree of Life: the cedar tree. Also known as Grandmother Cedar. The Tree of Life provides the channel of communication between the two worlds above and below the earth and is a symbol of both strength and flexibility in adversity.

Underwater Panthers: beings who are related to the Star People and make their homes in lakes.

Visions: a combination social and educational experience in which the ghost-portion of an individual makes contact with the Atisokanak People while awake but in a trance-like state.

War in the Heavens: a time in the distant past when, according to oral tradition, the different Star People were at war with each other and in the process destroyed certain areas of the Earth.

Water Beings: Star People living in the Great Lakes area who communicate with human beings though telepathy.

westing: the process of the Soul's journey to the Atisokanak world at the time of the physical body's death.

Windigo: possibly a manito, or possibly a long-extinct animal who is also called "The Great Ice and Snow Monster." It was said to be able to possess its human victims.

world view: a comprehensive conception of the world from a specific standpoint.